The Indian Dimension

The Indian Dimension
Politics of Continental Development

ROMESH THAPAR

VIKAS PUBLISHING HOUSE PVT LTD
New Delhi Bombay Bangalore Calcutta Kanpur

VIKAS PUBLISHING HOUSE PVT LTD
5 Ansari Road, New Delhi 110002
Savoy Chambers, 5 Wallace Street, Bombay 400001
10 First Main Road, Gandhi Nagar, Bangalore 560009
8/1-B Chowringhee Lane, Calcutta 700016
80 Canning Road, Kanpur 208004

ISBN 0 7069 0538 5

1V02T1201

Rs 40

Printed at Dhawan Printing Works, Mayapuri, New Delhi-110064

for
RAJ
and for reasons
well known to her

Contents

1   *Gandhi's Truth and Non-Violence*   1
2   *Jawaharlal Nehru in the Fight for National Independence*   8
3   *Freedom and Planning*   21
4   *National Interests—Options and Compulsions*   31
5   *Dynamic Centrism*   45
6   *Emerging Pattern of Politics and Leadership*   49
7   *Cleansing the Elections*   57
8   *Conformism*   62
9   *Perspectives on the Press*   68
10 *Political Theories and Practices*   74
11 *The 'Bandh' Business*   83
12 *Administration*   90
13 *Poverty of Nations or Notions*   97
14 *Wanted : An Integrated Society*   109
15 *Social and Distributive Justice*   115
16 *The Mass Line*   120
17 *Communications and Changing Values*   126
18 *Contradictions in Co-existence*   132
19 *After the China Clash*   136
20 *Asian Situation*   145
21 *Politics of Power*   153
22 *Our Security Scenario*   165
23 *Foreign Policy*   171
24 *Watershed Year*   179
25 *A Strategy for India*   186

1

Gandhi's Truth and Non-violence*

We have to look at Mohandas Karamchand Gandhi against the sweep of history and in the context of his Indian being, not as some kind of saint in search of impossibles. I belong to a generation deeply influenced by the events which Gandhi crystallized. I would, therefore, prefer to see him in the setting of political leadership, unique in many respects, particularly in terms of the ends and means.

Not so long ago, in colonial Asia the thinking man was inevitably the victim of a series of traumatic experiences, direct and otherwise. Either these experiences reduced him to voiceless servitude or they created in him the fertilizing ferment of revolt. Interestingly enough, Gandhi had see-sawed between both positions. In this sense, he was typical of the generation which rose to consciousness in the bloody years of the First World War and the revolutionary echoes of October 1917.

Gandhi the Hindu, the Indian, the Asian, the British subject, the humanist, realized early in life that a mechanical, unthinking approach to the problems of oppressed peoples, particularly the complex societies of the Indian subcontinent, would be

*This text comprises interventions made at the UNESCO International Roundtable held in Paris to mark the Gandhi Centenary in 1969. The theme was "Truth and Non-Violence in Gandhi's Humanism."

self-destructive. He sought meaningful alternatives which would be an integral part of his fundamental humanism.

It was only natural, therefore, that in his search for a philosophy of action, of fulfilment, Gandhi should immerse himself in the extraordinary richness of Hindu thought. In discussing Gandhi, Hinduism is a vital element—Hinduism that is a civilized, humane way of life, not a religion, not a ritual-encrusted system or something based on the edicts of rigid law-givers. Interestingly enough, Gandhi's innate humanism discovered in Hinduism two distinct streams of thought. First, the unending search for the Truth. "You are God," said the texts. "Be true unto yourself," was the invocation. In other words, the quantum of untruth is the quantum of your failure to be true to yourself. It was a doctrine of supreme individualism, of personal salvation. Second, the power of the commitment to non-violence which the Buddha had bequeathed to the land of his birth.

These two concepts—truth and non-violence—Gandhi saw as relevant to the universe. But they had to be forged into a weapon of action, for, without action, without change, nothing would survive. That weapon was *satyagraha*, a non-violent act of truth where the individual becomes part of the collective, where personal salvation is in the salvation of community, where moral force conditions the relationship between oppressor and oppressed, where no final answers are asserted, only an end is pursued. The "small voice within" joins, in a moment of truth, other small voices. Ends and means fuse, enrich each other. In other words, a general philosophy becomes an ethic of political action.

Truth and non-violence, in the context of Hindu philosophy, are necessarily different concepts than when they are placed in the setting of the Christian ethic. Hinduism does not nurture itself in eternal rights and wrongs. Its philosophy lies in the grey lands between the black and white of wrong and right. Only if we look upon Gandhi's thought in this setting which was integral to him, will we be able to understand the contradictions, the ambivalences, the dogmatisms and the commitments of one who never ceased his experiments. This was the essence of the man and his life.

It would be inaccurate to suggest or imply that Gandhi evolved certain principles of political, economic and social action and then applied them to India. The first experiments in Africa were to be profoundly conditioned by the realities of the Indian situation. If we were to distil the major considerations which marked Gandhi's strategy and tactics of mass action, we would discover that the principles which had been experimented with had great relevance to the demands of the Indian situation. The concept of *ahimsa* (non-violence), *satyagraha* (the struggle for truth) and *swadeshi* (self-reliance), provided the ingredients of an amalgam for India's liberation as a united, secular, democratic, egalitarian society. These were the purified means to serve a noble end. In Gandhi's view, a compromise on the means would only shatter the end in sight.

Let me explain in greater detail. When Gandhi resolved to lift the struggle of the Indian people for freedom from the quagmire of elitist constitutionalism to the plane of mass action, he put his ideas to systematic tests and linked them closely with what he perceived to be the key realities of the Indian situation. What were these realities?

The unity of a multi-faceted subcontinent obsessed him. Every political undertaking had to cherish this fragile unity. It could not be taken for granted. A whole subcontinent, with its many culture patterns, would have to be stirred into a symphony of action if this unity was to be preserved. Neglect of this or that region, or this or that community, would shatter the mosaic of this unity. Non-violence was a vital cement for the preservation of unity.

Closely linked to this concept of unity was the equally imperative need to somehow bridge the extraordinary gulf between a colonially sponsored elite and a down-trodden people. A new elan would have to be created through the instruments of struggle. Again those means and ends!

And, finally, the enemy was British Imperialism—powerful, capable of the usual brutalities associated with over-lordship, but sensitive to moral pressures because of a lively democratic conscience at home. This was not an unimportant consideration in planning the non-violent liberation of India. Moral force, as symbolized in *satyagraha*, could be a powerful weapon against an oppressor with a democratic conscience. Gandhi never lost sight of these three facets of the Indian situation while planning his *satyagraha* based on *ahimsa* and *swadeshi*.

Imagine what a different Gandhi would have emerged if India had been a compact single-nation State under the jackboot of a fascist power. The exercise is worth the trouble, because we are interested in the relevance of Gandhian techniques in a world which, despite its aberrations, is moving towards an enlightenment of the spirit of man.

Gandhi was no romantic. He was a most skilled and astute political leader of men. He advanced a thesis of revolt which captured the age-old dream of the Indian mind. He died convinced that he had failed but he had in fact sown a seed which would sprout in many lands, in many mutations—indeed, and this is important, wherever man still listened to that "small voice within."

Political liberation was the vast envelope for Gandhi's other experimental attitudes. Economic liberation was to come through *swadeshi* or self-reliance; and if this made the Indian rich richer, the concept of trusteeship was projected. The Hindu caste system was not denounced, only untouchability was treated as a disease. Religious tolerance was vital to India, but the tolerance was Hinduistic, born out of a centuries-old tradition to absörb and assimilate. Education was to be basic, linked to everyday needs, not designed to create men and women who would shatter orthodoxy, proclaim the reign of rationality, of science and technology geared to the growth of an enlightened society.

I call these attitudes experimental because Gandhi necessarily had to design every concept or theory to serve the goal of liberation. He could not risk, in the course of the freedom struggle, the popularization of concepts which would polarize the movement, create ideological rifts and threaten unified action over a complex subcontinent. The bullets of the assassin were, however, to deny us the opportunity to experience the flowering of Gandhian precept and practice in the years of freedom.

Of course, some will argue that Gandhi was always free to do what he willed. But this is far from the truth. Like any other, he was impacted deeply by considerations flowing from the struggle for freedom. We must, therefore, look to his universalism to discover the ideas which he was unable to apply. I believe that these would have sharply modified his thinking on economic liberation, social non-discrimination, religious tolerance and the education for the future. His dramatic appeal to the leaders and activists of the Indian National Congress, at their moment of triumph, to abjure power and to turn to the people to serve them carried within it a germinal concept.

The centenary is observed internationally because Gandhi today has wider influence than when he led the people of India. His ideas have crossed the many frontiers of our sadly divided world and are now enriching the techniques by which man either proceeds to assault the last vestiges of oppression or makes clear that he is a master of his political, economic and social situation.

In this connection, it is important that we recognize a major fact of our time: the incredible advance of science and technology which in its sweep takes man to the moon, has shrunk this world of ours. Distance rapidly ceases to have meaning. As the age of mass travel takes shape, the full impact of this fact will begin to be appreciated.

For the first time the phrase, "Family of Man," has valid meaning. Already one can discern a new humanism percolating into the consciousness of man. The Black and the White, the Brown and the Yellow have many psychological barriers to overcome. Battles will be fought to force these changes. But, it is clear that the "family" and its collective conscience is, at last, in the making.

If this assertion of the growth of a new family and a new humanism is accepted, it follows very naturally that truth and non-violence—whether perceived in Hindu terms or Christian—will play an increasingly positive role in our affairs as concepts to be developed and built upon.

Admittedly, a great deal of confusion will persist on these terms. After all to many, truth is absolute and non-violence is meaningless when violence is willed upon oneself as in Gandhi's *satyagraha*. There will be variations on the Gandhian theme. Indeed, it will even be argued that guerrilla action is controlled violence and to be preferred to head-on collisions. Whatever the argumentation, there will be broad agreement that, in a shrinking world, where various peoples are coming closer together in mutual respect and understanding, the techniques of non-violent struggle will be more relevant than those of traditional violence.

Confrontations disciplined by non-violence create, in the setting of a scientific and technological world which is capable of destroying itself in a single, violent exchange, a base of mass commitment and involvement which can seldom be matched by the system behind violent confrontations. This mass commitment and involvement restores to ordinary men and women the right of individual and collective power, individual and collective sovereignty. This, then, becomes the engine of progress, of social transformation.

Ironically, the Gandhian techniques of struggle become inspirational because the forward thrust of science and technology creates an antipathy to democratic functioning in those who lead this thrust. The dangers inherent in the concentration of power in the hands of the technologically and scientifically skilled will soon be on the agenda of the human race. Mass commitments and involvements, generated by the passion and courage inherent in non-violent confrontations, will provide a major corrective to any authoritarianism parading as the ultimate truth.

It is for this reason that Gandhian notions on the decentralization of power need to be more fully grasped. The assumption that these notions are rooted in some kind of anarchist perspectives is unfair to one who was deeply disturbed by the fate of man in this exciting, traumatic century.

Obviously, decentralization would condition the shape of the base of society and its superstructure. The emphasis would be on simple living and communal enjoyment—the only real weapons of the urban and rural proletariat against elites wedded to wasteful, irrelevant, personalized standards of living. Gandhi was convinced that a concentration of power in our present-day scientific and technocratic world would serve only elitist interests, polarize peoples, destroy the humanistic contest of living and unleash violence of a kind hitherto unknown. His was a groping towards a total, comprehensive view of man's condition and the framework within which this condition could be made healthy and purposeful.

We must, in other words, bring the detachment of non-violent truth to the study of Gandhi. Only then will we be able to sublimate the essence of his life and practice and draw valid lessons

for the struggle against injustice and war today. Artificial con-
tinuums should not be sought. Nor should dogmas be paraded
as inviolable. I say this because the cultists are easy to spawn.
Gandhi was rooted in the life around him. His thought and
practice was forever tested against real problems. His mind was
never closed. Small wonder that the complexity of his moves
baffled even those who were close to him.

It is in this spirit that Gandhi should be studied.

2

Jawaharlal Nehru in the Fight for National Independence*

We live in a historical period of profound economic and political transformations where many institutions are in flux, where
a phenomenal growth of science and technology are changing
the known contours of our accepted world. We must open many
doors to understand how men like Nehru moved millions into
action, moulded events, directed our thrust forward into the
future. It is in this spirit—the spirit of our times—that I have
approached Nehru's role in the fight for national independence
and international peace.

In India, from the early beginnings of modern political and
social action, we have witnessed repeated attempts to unravel
the Indian reality. It was part of the inner struggle of sensitive,
enlightened men to find communion with their people from
whom they were separated by an almost unbridgeable spiritual
and physical gulf. The unchanging village societies of a subcontinent seemingly defied understanding. Rammohan Roy,
Vivekananda, Bankim Chandra, and Gokhale were among the
giants who launched upon the building of a bridge, but the effort
was largely incomplete. Failing to achieve an equation with the
people, these outstanding men sought in comparative alienation

*This article was prepared for the International Round-table on
Jawaharlal Nehru organized by UNESCO in New Delhi in 1966.

the introspective world of personal salvation. Over the decades, the gulf widened.

When the young Jawaharlal returned to his country, he was already in the throes of this inner struggle. A love of country and people was not enough. Nor was nationalism fed by the British colonial presence. Indeed, circumstances almost pushed him into the civil service, and, later, into the lucrative legal profession of his father. This had been the fate of most of the elite. Nehru's search for the means with which to expel imperialism from his land should be seen in the context of his struggle to link with his people, to be able to understand their hopes and fears and to lead them to their dreams. Like so many before him, this modern, rational, impatient man must have been aware that alone, as an individual, he would become irrelevant in the terrifying vastness and complexity of India. Someone would have to help him "belong."

And that someone had arrived on the Indian scene, that rare prophet who at last possessed the key to the ethos of our people—Gandhiji. Nehru's almost immediate alliance with Gandhi was not accidental. Gandhi was lifting the freedom movement from the individual responses of the elite to the plane of mass action. He was also evolving the technique of non-violent, disciplined *satyagraha* which held out the hope that mass action would not end in chaos. Here was an intensely practical man, consciously applying his theories to the Indian reality, testing and re-testing them, determined to make the village his base. The bridge at last seemed complete. Significance entered Nehru's life.

Too little attention is paid to the framework of Nehru's thinking within the contours of the Indian reality which Gandhi sketched for him—and for so many others whom he moulded into heroic dimensions. In the relationship between these two extraordinary men, at a critical moment in the history of the nation, do we find the key to comprehending not only the men but the dynamics which were to condition the struggle for freedom, sustaining the faith of the people in ultimate victory despite the odds.

Gandhi was only too aware that a prolonged and violent struggle for power could dismember India's frail unity, held together in a modern sense by the mechanics of colonial exploitation—a unity that never really existed in history. He set out not only to strengthen the unifying factors in Indian life, but also to evolve a form of struggle which would preserve unity. *Ahimsa, satyagraha, and swadeshi* were the amalgam of Gandhi's "magic," a magic born of a deep understanding of our people, of our basic characteristics. It dissolved fears of fratricidal strife, gave the people the courage to stand up and challenge imperialism without weapons, and held out the threat of economic sanctions against the foreign exploiter. And, in the process, a varied assortment of men and women, belonging to various communities, classes and culture patterns, found themselves part of a common image. They, at last, could become a nation.

The practical, perceptive Gandhi was deeply conscious that the momentum of the non-violent struggle could not be sustained to the finish in the manner of a fight. The battle for freedom, to succeed in unity and non-violence, would have to proceed through phases, compromises, advances and retreats, until the whole country was moving in unity—the vertical ascent could only proceed by elaborate horizontal adjustment. But a complex struggle of this kind could only be conducted successfully if the pressure of public opinion in the world could be brought to bear upon the conscience of democratic Britain. That Britain was sensitive to such pressure was important; for a fascist state would have unleashed violent reactions and probably compelled a totally different response, changing the course of the unified struggle.

Shrewdly, over the years, Gandhi saw his ally in Nehru, the fighter for international causes who viewed the future of his country as an integral part of the world community. Always, Jawaharlal was his mentor on the world. And he was Jawaharlal's when India was on the agenda. They interpreted history differently, but that did not matter. If the struggle for freedom within the country was dominated by the incredible power of Gandhi's will, it had the inspiring sweep of Nehru's international commitments abroad. Two amazingly contrary men fused, as it were, in the mind of India. A deep communion was established between Sabarmati Ashram and Anand Bhavan.

The debates during the twenties, thirties and forties within the leading cadre of the Indian National Congress make very great sense when read and understood within this kind of framework. While Nehru, with his modern, scientific, socialist think-

ing worked for the radicalization of the movement, he was at
critical moments repeatedly persuaded to compromise with the
realistic traditionalism of Gandhi. It had become apparent to
both men that if the momentum and unity of the freedom
struggle was to be preserved they would have to work together.
The one could not really do without the other. Inevitably, over
the years, whether at home or abroad, Gandhi and Nehru were
complementary to an understanding of the Indian reality. The
compromises gave the Indian National Congress its strangely
amorphous character. Amorphousness was strength in the situation which prevailed over a sprawling and varied subcontinent
with its many developed communities, castes and interests seeking a national personality. An assembly of the Indian people
was what the Congress attempted to become—and became.
Impatience among his comrades was Gandhi's greatest fear.
Compromises, he realized, intensified this impatience. The clash
of developing and ramified interests, particularly the communal,
made compromise—and patience—harder to sustain.

Nehru was impatient. How often he exploded in despair or
in anger. With many millions on the move, and mass organizations straining at the leash, he could see the possibilities of a
dramatic overthrow of British power. But Gandhi always expended great effort to control him, pacify him, warning him of the
repercussions to national cohesion and unity, of hasty action. A
complex country had created within Nehru a dilemma which
was to remain with him to the end.

Nehru's compromises with Gandhi's thought and action cut
him off increasingly from his natural militant-nationalist, socialist
and communist allies in the movement. One by one, they with-
drew to pursue their own paths. Each was to be isolated by the
skill of Gandhi, the inspirational work of Nehru and the hard
organizing of the men who worked the machine of the movement which was quietly taking on in the forties the recognizable form of a party. Indeed, it was becoming a party fearful
of its own radicalism and encrusted with conservative responses.
Nehru's impatience grew rapidly with the crystalization of
Muslim separateness—and there seemed no reasonable solution
for it so long as the British remained on the scene.

In those momentous days which saw the defeat of fascism and
were to witness a transfer of power in India, he must have

wondered whether the patience of the Mahatma was the answer to India's unity—particularly when the armed forces began to stir under the impact of the naval strike in Bombay. The so-called Nehruites were impatient with Nehru. After all, significantly, the day after the start of the naval strike, a war-exhausted Britain announced the despatch of a Cabinet Mission to arrive at a final settlement of the Indian problem. Was this the time to talk or to fight? History is made in lonely decisions of this kind.

There were two possibilities at that moment in history—to continue on the basis of Gandhi's well-tested methods of compromise and adjustment and proceed with infinite patience to a gradual erosion of imperial power, or to adopt the more dramatic alternative, quickened as it was by the traumatic events of world history (the triumph over fascism and the inspiring victories of the peoples struggles), and call for a revolutionary leap to a predetermined uprising and the overthrow of alien rule. As we now see it, neither alternative worked. Caught within the constitutional web of the cleverest imperial power the world has known, and confronted basically by the main contradictions of Gandhi and Nehru in their purest abstract sense, the country was impelled towards partition, towards a tragic finale to the freedom struggle.

The compromise of partition was rooted essentially in impatience, impatience with the parochial and the bigotted who refused to work for unity, impatience with the patience of those who believed that only through prolonged and disciplined struggle could unity be preserved, impatience to expel the British from India, impatience to take charge of the country and get it moving. Gandhi was patient. He could not accept the vivesection of India. His dream of unity was defeated almost at the moment of triumph—or so he thought.

History might well conclude, when all the facts are known, that Gandhian patience could have compelled an exhausted Imperial Britain to hand over power to a united centre a few years later. Nehru, emotionally opposed to partition, must have played with the same thoughts, but the immediate compulsions were irresistible. A chain of events had been set in motion. The whole structure of imperial power was breaking up. Even the princes were dreaming—of power! There was a gnawing fear that delay would certainly spark uncontrollable extremism, communal, feudal and secular, which even an exhausted alien ruler could exploit for further vivesection of the subcontinent. The pointers were visible to all. Violence was in the air.

Freedom came. And with it, a divided and explosive heritage. Within months, came the biggest blow of all: the inevitable, inexplicable climax to partition. An assassin's bullets silenced the man who had been Nehru's living link with the India he so passionately loved. Many years earlier, writing about Gandhi, Nehru had unconsciously revealed the meaning to him of this link:

> He is an extraordinary paradox. I suppose all outstanding men are so to some extent. For years I have puzzled over this problem: Why with all his love and solicitude for the underdog he yet supports a system which inevitably produces it and crushes it; why with all his passion for non-violence he is in favour of a political and social structure which is wholly based on violence and coercion. Perhaps it is not correct to say that he is in favour of such a system; he is more or less a philosophical anarchist. But as the ideal anarchist state is too far off still and cannot easily be conceived, he accepts the present order. It is not, I think, a question of means, that he objects, as he does, to the use of violence in bringing about a change. Quite apart from the methods to be adopted for changing the existing order, an ideal objective can be envisaged, something that is possible of achievement in the not distant future. Sometimes he calls himself a socialist, but he uses the word in a sense peculiar to himself which has little or nothing to do with the economic framework of society which usually goes by the name of socialism. Following his lead, a number of Congressmen have taken to the use of the word, meaning thereby a kind of muddled humanitarianism. I know Gandhiji is not ignorant of the subject, for he has read many books on economics and socialism and even Marxism, and has discussed it with others. *But I am becoming more and more convinced that in vital matters the mind by itself does not carry us far . . .*

From his lonely summit of power, Jawaharlal Nehru was soon to sense his own perceptive power to analyze and dissect the tangled skein of the reality that had emerged in free India. In essence it was an inheritance from Gandhi, but he had woven into it his own sensitive rediscovery of his land and people. In the course of the freedom struggle and the tentative planning of India's free future, he had convinced himself that the political energy of a complex society in the throes of fundamental development is dependent on understanding the role of a host of contrary factors and how the three conditioners of change—the inert, the catalyst and the polarizer—are brought into some kind of creative partnership. The unity of India obsessed him, for India was poor, backward, obscurantist and could be chopped up into many pieces under external and internal pressures. He set out to elaborate for his countrymen the conceptual disciplines which would provide the frame for political-economic growth in unity.

Operating on a large time scale, with a dedication which was to become legendary, Nehru tested and re-tested his ideas and finally reduced them to what he thought would be the ever-present conditioning influences. First, the very sensitive federal character of our state which dictates a responsive, continental balance of power between the various regions. Second, the powerful, persistent assertion of the regional elites and specialized interests that an equal sharing of economic resources be the basis of national development. And, third, the pressure to defend the people's aspirations, and, through secular safeguards, the essential interests of the many and sizeable communities inhabiting the state, particularly those which exist continentally and which help strengthen the bonds of federal unity. These influences were translated by him into the slogans of democracy, socialism and secularism and he repeatedly warned that we could only neglect them at our peril.

Democracy in our country, Nehru maintained, is not just a matter of exercising the vote in freedom and secrecy, or of electing governments every five years. Indian democracy must possess the special capacity to cushion, amend or mould regional demands in a way that they do not erode the unity and strength of the federal structure. It must also be capable of curbing regionalism, particularly when the interests of the more powerful (or the less powerful) take on arrogant, chauvinistic postures in linguistic, caste and communal agitations with their markedly

economic-political dimensions. And all this sophisticated adjustment must be achieved in conditions where both politics and
economics are underdeveloped.

Socialism in our conditions, Nehru emphasized, is not concerned only with building up the public sector of the economy
to a commanding position, and with curbing the profit and privilege of the more affluent in our developing society. Indian
socialism demands that urgent attention be paid to the backward areas of the country. A limited economic cake has to be
divided in a planned manner so that every region feels that it
has a stake in the business of growth planning. This is not as
easy as it sounds, for unrealistic regional demands can lead to
uneconomic spending and a declining growth rate despite the
mobilization effort put in. Many an economic posture will have
to be dictated by the fusion or clash of regional interests. Political leadership cannot ignore these economic equations.

Secularism, Nehru underlined, is not designed only to assure
the peace and security of the minorities, or of the Muslims in
particular. It demands that we renounce Hindu revivalism, that
integration between the communities take place through the
processes of industrial and technological growth, that there be
full recognition and respect for difference and non-conformity.
In other words, any attempt artificially to create what is known
as a single-nation State be discouraged, for, such an attempt
would only undermine a growing federal unity.

Nehru was convinced that democracy, socialism and secularism understood in the Indian context place a heavy responsibility on the central power which must combine the functions of
a disciplining force, a safety valve, a consensus-maker and a
pace-setter. He was equally convinced that any weakening of
the central power on these crucial concepts of our federal polity
generates the kind of tensions which disrupt the smooth functioning of the State. This conviction motivated Nehru to make
a conscious and continuing effort at the regional and central
level to structure Indian unity within the dynamics of a national
consensus—the maximum possible. A total confrontation between Right and Left was sought to be blunted.

It could be argued that this approach emerged from a very
special appreciation of reality by Nehru. Here, perhaps, we
might eventually seek his permanent relevance in history. It

makes him in a way more of a moral philosopher than a pragmatic innovator in political strategy. His deep commitment to Gandhi's Indianness categorically rules out violence as a means. To him, the poet and the philosopher, life in all its manifestations takes on a profound spiritual meaning, even an idyllic, almost romantic, mysterious significance. He had seen the dogmas fail. Yet the terrible poverty of his people would not allow him personal salvation. He therefore conceived of institutional change with a conscious acceptance of delay. Change was no longer to be measured by speed alone. Only that change was worthwhile which would change man. The objective of a socialist society had to be measured by the exercise of individual morality. That this poetic, audacious, almost romantic concept of transformation was to be attempted by the world's poorest people was ironic. Therefore, this thinking needed translation into strategy.

As it evolved, this Nehruist strategy—in many respects similar to the theorising on a single party system in other parts of Asia and Africa but without the rigidity of encirclement which an authoritarian form imposes—fortified the original character of the Indian National Congress (that is, an amorphous assembly of varied opinions) and prepared it for the challenges born out of freedom. Even opposition parties, including those with an apparently revolutionary intention, began in one way or another to subscribe to the politics of consensus. The job of the ruling leadership was to forge a relevant, forward-looking maximum consensus. The job of the radical opposition outside was to prevent the forging of a minimum consensus which could be dictated by the entrenched, conservative elements of the ruling party. Political battles assumed the form of family quarrels, a breakdown or erosion of the national consensus only taking place when a particular plateau of development was reached and vested interests stood in the way of forward movement or the ascent to the next plateau; in other words, a readjustment of the horizontal components for a new consensus. It was a remarkable achievement, expressing itself fully in the optimistic fifties, an achievement comparable to the "magic" of Gandhi's *ahimsa*, *satyagraha* and *swadeshi*. It raised a whole nation to its feet and gave it the confidence to move towards a modern world after centuries of slumber. It identified him totally with the people.

The national consensus was projected internationally, too. Non-alignment, as enunciated by Nehru and backed fully by his people, gradually came to be accepted as an immensely powerful weapon for the emerging independent nations of Asia and Africa. Indeed, it was regarded as the measure of a new nation's independence in international affairs. Nehru did not evolve his attitudes through "hunches." He applied his mind to the harsh realities of a cold war situation and thrashed out an approach which would serve the national interest of India which he saw as closely interlocked with the fate of embattled Asia and Africa.

When India gathered her strength in freedom, the world was apprehensive, uncertain of the future. A terrible war had ended. Another was threatened by the "arrival" of the nuclear age. Nehru, nourished on the humanistic, liberal thought of the west and the egalitarian, anti-imperialist ideology of the socialist communist movement, saw a world divided dangerously into two blocs. He realized that commitment either way would sharpen the existing polarization, increase the chances of war and gravely damage the possibility of the developed world aiding the underdeveloped which constituted two-thirds of mankind. He had to move cautiously, for neutralism was suspect in a sharply divided world and, if amateurishly enunciated, could isolate India.

Starting with an assessment of the geographical position of India and its size, the fact that it could not be ignored for long by either of the power blocs, that we would have a common frontier with the communist world, that a democratic society would always have to embody the elements of a mixed economy—whether of private and public sector or public sector and cooperative sector—rooted in a socialist base, that India's many communities and culture patterns, some advanced and some backward, would necessitate a system of balanced economic planning, Nehru could turn on his unthinking critics and ask them what policy other than a neutral or non-aligned one truly reflected the national interest. The internal compulsions dictated the external posture. The external posture assisted the transformation of internal realities in the direction of a planned polity which would seek a democratic, secular and socialist structure.

But there was something more to it. This policy did not interpret national self-interest as transitory opportunism. It was again
an expression of Nehru's extremely moral central position—
that man must resolve problems in tolerance, without violence,
in a kind of consensus and, above all, his action must be illumin-
ed by possibilities for the future of man. On the sensitive peri-
pheries of the cold war confrontation, this faith was put under
heavy strain but it did in a way condition Nehru's position.
Tibet was a vaccum which had to be filled—and China had the
greater right to fill it. If there was bloodshed in Hungary, and
the suppression of a popular revolt, attitudes were to be fashioned not in simple principles but in the need for the time being to
stabilize the confrontation between the blocs. He believed firmly
that normality returns to revolutions, and always viewed the
angry outbursts of neighbouring China in this context. If he was
compelled to adopt postures towards the latter part of his life
which were dictated largely by national self-interest, it was only
a short-term necessity. He seldom lost sight of the perspectives
he had sketched. This approach lifted the concept of non-alignment to a positive philosophy for many countries of the world
and provided the opportunity to stabilize the confrontation of
the super-powers. It was in perfect accord with the ethos of his
people who did not see things in black or white, but in shades
of grey.

The main strategic aim of the non-aligned nations, brought
together by the persuasive faith of Nehru, was therefore to
arrange a *detente* between the two hostile blocs. This could only
be achieved through a *detente* between the bloc leaders. The
collective power of the non-aligned was brought into play at
various levels, including the United Nations. The grim logic of
the nuclear age, and the wider recognition of the consequences
of a nuclear clash, gave voice to the demand for a *detente* within the blocs. It isolated, and at the same time excited, the sectarians in both blocs to oppose this trend for peace as a betrayal
of principles. Nehru was to invite the wrath of the sectarians
of the world, but, undaunted, almost Gandhian in resolve, he
pursued his objective of peace among men.

"In dreams begin responsibilities." Fulfilment awaits another
day. If Mahatma Gandhi's vision of a united India was darken-
ed in 1947 by the partition of the subcontinent, Jawaharlal

Nehru's determination to lift his land and people into the twentieth century was blunted in 1962 by a developing military confrontation along India's sprawling frontier which brought into sharp focus the weaknesses, the gaps, and the shortfalls in the economic and political effort during the years of freedom. The spirit of India sagged, despite the massive achievements of these years.

We are too close to these events to take even the beginnings of an objective historical view. Questions crowd the mind. Did Nehru's obsession with the formulation of a unifying consensus create a dependence on a continuum which, among other things dictated that a colonial-type apparatus of administration perform complex tasks for which it was unsuited? If the consensus on policy forged by Nehru embodied the broad support of almost every political party in the country, what prevented a fuller involvement and commitment of his natural allies outside the Congress Party? Was it the tendency in the ruling party to exclusivity in the exercise of power which drove away the talent which alone could operate the impressive superstructure for the speedy democratic socialist transformation of India? Or had the world's experience of the aberrations of political organization made Nehru inhibited, fearful of becoming a captive of supposedly dedicated party cadres who were urgently needed as implementors of policy? Or did growth in a mixed economy create other powerful vested interests capable of opposing a revolutionary breakthrough? Had the economic and political pulls of the twentieth century made it imperative to design a sharper weapon of transformation and renewal than the consensus of a Gandhi or a Nehru? The answers to these questions cannot undermine the unique contribution of Jawaharlal Nehru to his country's entry into the twentieth century, but they will inevitably determine national attitudes in the years to come.

By 1962, the threat to the frontiers of India eroded the internal consensus; defence had become a crippling burden and was polarizing political and economic attitudes. Externally, the patient work for world peace done on the basis of non-alignment was fractured. Confusion and discord set in to take their toll. But, undaunted to the very end, Jawaharlal Nehru searched for the answers to the questionings in the mind of India. It is even possible to speculate that he was reaching out for a deeper

exploration of his concepts, crossing the boundaries of India
towards a greater continental balance and unity. When we think
of him, we shall always remember him as one who never ceased
to search for the pathways to India's unity, to India's upliftment
from centuries of poverty, to India's spiritual renaissance in a
world where sensitive men would live in peace and concord.

3

Freedom and Planning*

In a sense the story of the world is the story of man's effort to enlarge the boundaries of freedom. Yet, ironically enough, the basic mechanisms of modern society are a threat to this freedom. Our technological age, by its very nature, is placing more and more power in the hands of small groups of specialists. The average citizen is increasingly unable to comprehend the ramifications of the society in which he lives; he interests himself in his own small activities and is only too willing to leave larger issues to be solved by supposedly encyclopaedic minds.

The danger inherent in such a situation is underlined by the increasing power of the State and private monopoly to influence minds which have ceased to think or which have lost the capacity to disagree. Dissent becomes rarer and rarer. Conformity is the new value of the mid-twentieth century.

If we pause to assess human advance the problem becomes clear. Our achievement, over the past twenty years, in the fields of science and technology could be equated to the giant strides taken during the previous 200 years. And what was accomplished in the seventeenth and eighteenth centuries was far greater than perhaps the entire progress of man before that time, a recorded history of some 5,000 years. But man's mind, the capacity to solve the new social and organizational challenges, has not been able to keep up with this dramatic advance.

*From *Seminar* 3, November 1959.

This is certainly the crucial contradiction of our times, a contradiction which is likely to sharpen from year to year, from day to day, as the stars pass from the realm of poetry to the reach of man, as we burst into space seeking the shores of new planets.

Against this background, India and other underdeveloped countries, where two-thirds of the world's population receives one-sixth of the world's income, are attempting, through State-led economic planning, to make up within decades, the leeway of centuries. They must hurry or else remain underdeveloped and backward, and lose the benefits of scientific and technological advances. Here, more and more, the State is being invested with overriding powers exercised by a bureaucracy that multiplies endlessly. Can man escape the results of this concentration of power? If so, how? Are the democratic processes strong enough to safeguard freedom of thought and expression? Can we save ourselves from the clutches of conformity?

These questions assume different proportions in the various countries of the underdeveloped world. They are not understood really by the political philosophers of advanced nations. In the west, for example, a most developed industrial and technological base exists already. It has the capacity to meet the high consumption needs of the population in farm and factory. In other words, such countries need only to organize more rationally their means of production and to make the distribution of wealth more equitable. For them it is not necessary to curb consumption drastically in order to create the surplus for rapid development, for what Subhas Chandra Bose once called "the forced march." Democratic traditions, already established firmly, do not hinder the business of reorganization, but assist the process of building a more just and equitable society. Aberrations occur, disastrous at times, but a highly mechanized civilization gives rise to problems of individual freedom vastly different to ours.

In India, where people still live with starvation in sight, where the economy is emerging from a mass of feudal relations, where the means do not exist to support huge populations, and where the surplus for industry has to be created, the fear that planning will become increasingly totalitarian is valid. Dissent under such planning tends to become a burden. Let it wait until the minimum necessities of life are fulfilled!

Yet it is difficult to determine the dividing line between "acceptable" dissent and that which is not. The momentum of change from a life of starvation to a life of survival and to dreams of plenty is such that the voices of dissent are swept aside by voices of conformity. Full freedom is shelved. But can freedom wait? Can it be picked up after ten or twenty years of exile?

Experience of planned economies shows that democratic processes can be quickly forgotten. It is therefore important that we plan our freedom parallel with our plans for material prosperity. The two must be complementary. If thought and money can be expended on experiments, successful or otherwise, in the fields of science and technology, why should not the same be in the field of human relations, particularly to extend man's freedom?

We must first agree on the discipline which the exercise of real freedom inevitably involves. Much has been written on this subject, but we need to take the essence of it and apply it constructively to the Indian reality. Let us proceed step by step.

Freedom from unrepresentative government is the starting point of any effort to humanize our society. It is not enough that elections are held every four or five years, that the vote is secret and supposedly free. We must analyze not only the outward election trappings but what goes on openly or surreptitiously to bring pressure on the voter.

While we are spared the dubious benefits of mass communication media, we have to contend with illiteracy, caste, religious and regional affiliations—pressures which blur the outlines of contending economic, political and social policies and play on the primitive emotions of the electorate. As a result, representatives who are very often elected do not reflect the thought of their constituencies on the many problems that come up before Parliament and the State Legislatures.

Traditional group loyalties take long to wither, but in the meantime it is possible to counter the ill-effects of elections held under such conditions. The right to recall a representative must become part of our democratic procedure. If a majority in a particular constituency is sufficiently agitated to go through the business of affixing their signatures to such a demand, there seems no reason why the right should not be granted. The threat of recall might also sober those who win elections on minority votes in triangular contests. Similarly, any policy adopted by a government at the Centre or in the States which creates tension beyond the normal should become the subject for a referendum. The cost of such procedure is small, if properly organized, and certainly worthwhile in the interest of ordered progress.

The recognition of these rights will require their inclusion in the Constitution. This brings us to an aspect that most people tend to ignore. Our Constitution is remarkable in many ways, but it has been subjected to a series of amendments which offend its original spirit. While it is necessary to introduce new democratic features into it, any attempt to curtail those which already exist must be put to the popular vote. We cannot have party machines upsetting the rights embodied in the Constitution merely to achieve some temporary political objective, as is so often the case. Freedom from arbitrary government is, in fact, the right of a people to be ruled by a government of laws and not of men acting on their individual whims. Only then, too, will that other freedom—from arbitrary privilege whether of race or class—be assured.

We also need to reconsider seriously the validity in today's terms, of the parliamentary practices we have borrowed from the west, particularly since these may pose a threat to genuine democracy. For example, the system of open voting in the legislatures vitiates independent thinking and places tremendous coercive power in the hands of the party machine acting through its party whips. A secret vote, not difficult in this technological age, would more accurately reflect the sentiments of legislators. Such a procedure would not be denying citizens the opportunity of knowing how their representatives voted because it in no way reduces the legislator's ability to participate openly in the debate. Jekyll and Hyde characters would be few and far between.

Then, again, the present method of "filling" the Rajya Sabha defeats the purpose for which this Upper House was created. The original intention was that the Rajya Sabha should be composed of elder statesmen, individuals rich with experience who had distinguished themselves in various fields of activity and who were unlikely to face the strain and tension of an election campaign. Political parties were expected to nominate such persons to the Rajya Sabha but, on the contrary, the House has been packed with defeated candidates or elder politicians only fit for retirement. Obviously, it is not possible to legislate for the composition of the Rajya Sabha. Healthy precedents should be established, and in this the ruling party, whether at the Centre or in the States, can play a major role.

How is the personality cult to be dealt with in the political life of underdeveloped nations? We speak of ceilings on income and ceilings on land holdings, but why not a "ceiling" on the tenure of Presidents, Prime Ministers, Chief Ministers and Ministers? This interesting suggestion has already been mooted. Perhaps two terms should be the limit, representing a decade in the life of a nation. Compulsory retirement after two terms or a transfer from one political level to another would, as in every other professional activity, clear the way for younger elements, create new cadres of political leadership and help to solve the vexed problem of "succession."

Indeed, much needs to be done to make Parliament and the Legislatures more vigorous and vital. Any visitor to these fountainheads of power comes away sadly demoralized. Apart from the normal procedures, it is necessary to bring the people into closer day-to-day association with the work of these bodies. Various ways can be found to do this. For example, special parliamentary or assembly committees, composed of men and women who enjoy wide respect and trust, should always be available to hear serious grievances about the misuse of power, corruption and similar problems. The committees' proceedings should be in secret and held confidential. They should regularly report the gist of their findings to Parliament or the Legislatures, leaving the decision about further action to the Members of those bodies. If we proceed along these lines we must, at the same time, create conditions favourable to the free expression of opinion. Such conditions do not exist in India despite the Supreme Court, the High Courts and other judicial structures. What little dissent does find expression is being gradually muffled by a combination of forces which stem from State-led planning.

The businessman is afraid because he is dependent on the government for the grant of licences. The bureaucrat, with an eye on his career, takes the line of least resistance. The professionals see merit in being apolitical. The intellectuals and creative workers are determined to find a niche in the Akadamies, in government publishing concerns, and in official information and broadcasting services. The peasants are being slowly silenced by the ramifications of the community development administration which has large funds at its disposal. Only the industrial workers are still able to express themselves from time to time, but with the State in the process of becoming the "universal owner and employer" it is likely that they too will be muzzled "in the interests of national development."

At the moment we are experiencing only the beginning of the process of centralized planning. In other words, if political government over the years becomes the universal owner and the universal employer in the field of economic production, can the freedoms we cherish be maintained with our present system of checks and balances? There is truth in the saying that power can be restrained only by power. But what if one concentration of power becomes so all-embracing that no other power or combination of powers can stand against it? In such a situation, would it not be possible to formally accept the freedoms referred to above and yet make a mockery of them? In fact, this is what already happens in various ways in all societies, whether "planned" or "unplanned."

India is fortunate. She has begun her experiments in State-led economic planning at a time when a considerable amount of literature is available on the practical results of such techniques in other lands. It is only natural that she should imbibe this experience, learn from it and then apply it creatively to her own peculiar conditions. This is the time to experiment, when the organizational forms of the emerging planned society are still in a fluid state. Delay at this juncture would only lead to the mistakes, often grave, which others have committed.

To begin with, the whole question of "the tempo of advance" must be subjected to careful analysis. Clearly, the attempt to put everybody into a straight-jacket in order to achieve certain "targets" fixed arbitrarily by some distant group of men, who think they can do no wrong, is a barbaric and primitive approach to planning. The sort of planning necessary for under-developed countries has to be based on the effort which the people are prepared to put into it. Inspire them by all means to work fourteen hours a day, but do not prod them with threats. The dividing line between consent and dissent is thin, very thin. We must find ways and means to obtain a genuine popular reaction to planning "targets" and all that these inevitably involve.

Is it always necessary to fix the highest rate possible for capital formation and to insist on maximum austerity? Would a slower tempo of development satisfy the economic and social urges of the people and provide them with the standards of life which they seek? What are these standards? Must they be always based on the distorted patterns of the west? Do we not need to reassess regularly some of the basic dogmas on which we attempt to plan the future of society? These are only some of the questions that must be asked and answered. Surprisingly little thought is given to these aspects, although it is well known that minor mistakes in fixing targets and rates of development can lead to explosive results.

Clearly, if we are to advance with popular consent, planning must start from below—at the *panchayat* and factory level. While coordination and central direction are necessary for any plan implementation, these must be sensitive to advice from below. The overall plan must not be presented as an edict, as so often happens today. Initiative at local levels must be sought for and built up. All this requires a plan-conscious base.

Without such a base all claims that planning is democratic are fraudulent, and bound to lead to the most serious conse-quences. Whether the "Haves" like it or not they will have to submit to the urges of the "Have-nots"; the tension between these two broad and opposed sections would ease were the con-viction widespread that the finalized plan had overwhelming popular support. We are far from this goal, for even the planners at the top have little faith in their plans!

Once the plan has been worked out, then the question of its implementation raises new problems. Whether under total or partial planning conditions, these problems are similar. In the economic and social fields, as in all other fields, an effort has to be made to take forward and develop the positive aspects of past societies. It is agreed, and not without some justification, that planning techniques tend to destroy initiative and the benefits of competition, that a soulless bureaucracy can easily become a victim of its own statistics and targets, and that it is criminal to destroy those impulses in human beings which have over the past 200 years been the mainsprings of human endeavour. It should be possible for us in India to apply our minds to these problems.

For example, whenever the State enters a particular field of production, why does it always tend to establish a vast monolithic organization which, without a doubt, is obviously inspired by the worst features of monopoly capitalist economic organization? What prevents the planners from setting up a number of competing units in the same field? Surely this approach would lead to greater efficiency and maintain a healthy competition between the competing managements?

By this it is not intended to suggest some primitive-type competition over the fixing of targets; let the costing of goods, their design, quality and durability, the ability to meet the genuine needs of the market, be given free play. A start should be made in those sections of the economy where the State is the sole producer. A similar competition could be arranged in those industries where the private and public sector cater to the same market. All this requires careful working out, but there is no reason why we should despair of a solution.

In this connection, with the State becoming a major entrepreneur, it is necessary that the question of hours and wages, of workers' rights, be negotiated by organizations which cannot be manipulated by the State. Should not competing interests be represented by competing organizations? Does this create anarchy? If each side possesses a last-minute veto, would this not restrain an intoxicated bureaucracy and act as a powerful lever for negotiated and mutually-acceptable settlements?

These questions have of late been raised by political philosophers but there seems to be a tendency widely prevalent in India to avoid the trouble of finding the answers. Of course, it is easy for those who rule to dismiss these questions as unreal, yet it is clear that unless we find answers to them we shall be moving

towards a society very different from the one whose vague outlines gave us the original inspiration.

And this brings us to the crucial question of dissent. Upon
dissent is based the whole edifice of the freedom of expression,
of searching enquiry, of independent thought, of the effort to
locate the truths which evade us in this cosmic age. Without
dissent no society can really unravel the complexities of modern
life; in fact, any fundamental analysis of human progress would
indicate that only where dissent has been given free play,
whether in one field of activity or many, has it been possible to
develop creatively and build upon our limited knowledge of what
was, what is and what will be. To curb or suppress the voices of
dissent, even for a transitory period, is tantamount to damaging
the living thought processes which help in the development of
the total man.

Yet, how easily is dissent brushed aside, crushed or dismissed
on the plea that it is based on false promises and stems from
small, privileged or unrepresentative elements in society. This
may often be true, but why should the decision be left to politicians and bureaucrats, or the supervisory committees they create
to implement their policies? Why should not the people be given
a chance to do the deciding, particularly in those societies which
are socialist or striving to arrive at socialism?

It may well be maintained that in India the parliamentary
system and the existence of opposition parties ensure the right
of dissent. But that would be begging the question. Even in the
most democratic parliamentary societies, dissent is under constant pressure to surrender. What then of India where democratic
roots are young?

Even today, there is a marked tendency among those who do
use their brains and think to avoid the tribulations involved in
dissent and to bathe in official patronage. The whole of the
nation's life is beholden, in one way or another, to organizations
created or supported by the State. This is inevitable in a poor
country, and therefore all the more reason that Akadamies,
State publishing houses, book trusts, broadcasting networks,
theatres and the like should make room for dissenters; they
should, indeed, encourage dissent, for what use is intellectual
effort without it?

The danger signals are there for all to see: monolithic Akadamies, monolithic publishing houses and monolithic information services and book trusts; small coteries, with influential connections, for ever in-charge through skilful permutations and combinations; widespread favouritism and corruption sponsored indirectly and blessed by official subsidy and patronage; and many honest men and women, dissenters all, who keep their distance for fear of pollution. It is an unhappy state of affairs, made all the more unhappy by the fact that the "private sector" is almost as solid and monolithic too! Destroy dissent among the thinking sections of the population and you destroy it at every level. This is a truth that few dare challenge.

Here there is urgent need to introduce democratic forms and a competitive spirit. Let the members of Akadamies be elected through secret ballot by their professional colleagues. Let there be not one but several State publishing houses, book trusts, broadcasting networks and theatres in every region to compete for popular support. Let cooperatives be formed to break the deadening grip of those who monopolize the channels of communication. It is possible to organize such a democratic, competitive system even where the State is the universal employer. It requires effort—and if we don't put it in now we shall create problems not only for future generations but for ourselves.

The lazy pessimists will say that the cost of these experiments is too great. It is the favourite argument of the "do-nothings." Let us calculate the cost! Indeed, what are planners for if not to prepare exciting ideas on paper so that we may decide whether they are feasible or not. Too long have we wallowed in this business of borrowing the not-so-brilliant plans and policies of others. It is about time that we brought our own faculties into play. This is the moment to do it, when State-led planning is still in the formative stage and has not yet breached the defences of freedom.

4

National Interests—Options and Compulsions*

India is such a vast region that for any speaker to attempt any lecture on her is a problem. When I was given this rather sprawling subject to deal with, my first intention was naturally to try and bring it down to some kind of manageable proportion.

I can start with the obvious fact that all state policy is motivated by a given understanding of national interests. It is not so much the difference in interests but in how to devise a policy to serve them that is important. Within this context, it is best to start by detailing our national interests. I will try to explain to you this evening, how an Indian looks up to his interests and tries to relate them.

The frame is not what it is made out to be in the world's press and in the mass media. I will present you a frame which exists in the mind of every intelligent Indian and I hope that at the end of it I will not have confused you but assisted you in understanding how the Indian views these problems.

Let me begin by asking: what are India's national interests? Now, interestingly enough, the first and basic interest in the mind of the Indian is the unity of his country. This is an ex-

*This lecture was given at a Foreign Relations Dinner Address Meeting in Tokyo's International House in March 1969.

tremely strange statement because normally most nations accept unity as a fact. They are not obsessed with it. The unity of India is an obsession with the Indian because this unity is of recent vintage and it is to be very carefully nurtured. It cannot be taken for granted.

We are, as you all know, a federal State and this federal State comprises many highly developed communities. Each community has its past, its culture, its languages, its script. It is not as if one major community is artificially trying to raise the level of so many other communities. Indeed, sometimes, and now more frequently, with Communism asserting itself more and more in India, we are described as a multi-national State by the Communist Party (Marxist).

This unity which we speak of in India, which we think of and nourish, is, as I have said, of recent vintage, and this is despite all that you would normally read in the Indian papers about our ancient and medieval empires and the great traditions of India. This is so much nonsense in terms of historical fact. To some extent, our unity was created by a vague kind of Hindustani culture which evolved over the centuries. To some extent, it was enriched by shared experiences between the regions. To some extent, it was the result of the British imperial presence which demanded the consolidation of the most profitable colonial property possessed by it.

To cement this unity, this kind of Indianness, to give it a new modern character, was the major task of political leadership. And it remains its major task.

Secondly, there is the concept that this unity is a mosaic of rich variety, a variety that must be properly fused, meshed, "integrated" as the politicians say. This concept is based upon the understanding that there must be respect for difference, that conformism to the patterns dictated by a dominant group is a danger to the strength and viability of the State. In our situation this demands the disciplining—and I say this very consciously—disciplining of Hindu chauvinism as much as of regional chauvinism. Most literature on India speaks largely about regional chauvinism, regional demands. Very little of the literature speaks about Hindu chauvinism, the desire to make everybody conform to a single image. In India this is out. You have to accept and respect difference in others.

The third point which I would like to stress is the strengthening of this unity in economic terms. A vast subcontinent has to be developed in a balanced manner. The huge gulfs between town and village, between backward area and advanced area have to be consciously bridged by economic planning. They cannot be left to the free play of the market because the free play of the market permits a movement only towards areas which are developed. This development has to be conditioned, directed consciously in the interest of India unity. In other words, a very limited "cake" has to be very carefully divided among the constituents of a federal State. An unbalanced development, resulting from a free play of the market, would only generate serious tensions and explosions endangering the unity of the federal structure.

As you know, this is an extremely costly business in terms of economics, but it is a cost that we have to bear constantly, consistently, and for many years until the unity of India is absolutely crystallized and consolidated.

The fourth point I would like to stress is the need in the country, where many centuries are telescoped into one situation, one moment and are interlocked, the need to stress the paramount importance of modernization, the need to modernize traditional attitudes, to bring them abreast of scientific and technological dimensions. This transformation is absolutely necessary for carrying out a speedy development of resources and for freeing the natural initiatives of the people. It is also necessary for our internal and external self-reliance in a fast changing world. This is very easily said but extremely difficult in our continental conditions. The approach from one region to another region has to vary. It has to take note of so many factors, so many tensions, so many overlapping points of interest between the regions in order to unleash a feeling of unified movement.

For example, we have been doing a great deal in primary education. Within the next five years the whole country will be covered by primary education—free, compulsory primary education—but we have not been able to inject into primary education an adequate amount of modernization, an adequate amount of science and technology, even rural technology. We have not been able to do it. The result has been that the explosion of

education has become an explosion of traditionalism, and traditionalism itself becomes the block to political and economic
development. So education, which is supposed to fertilize development, very often becomes a block, and this is the kind of
problem that presents itself whever we undertake any development in India—a situation which demands from the thinkers in
India, the planners in India, a very much more total approach
in perspective to their problems.

And, finally, one other aspect of national interest is that our
thrust into the future has to be in peace and concord in democracy. We in India, as political scientists, as social scientists,
are absolutely convinced that there can be no autocratic
posturing. This would immediately spell danger to India's
unity which is still frail and has to be strengthened and consolidated. In other words, you cannot imagine any serious
political activity in India which is based upon a kind of "coupist"
approach. A coup in one part of the country would not have
relevance in another part of the country. The country is so large.
When we speak of India, it is necessary to speak of India
in terms of the size of Europe. The subcontinent has the same
kind of cultural differentiation as Europe. It has more languages.
It has more scripts. It today has more political parties enjoying
power, physical power, and it is run ultimately by a central
government. The achievement is not small, but it is based upon
this understanding that there can be no autocratic commitment
in India, that we have to proceed in democracy.

This is often sneered at. "These Indians," it is said "are
always talking about democracy." I apologize for Indians who
speak about democracy as if they invented it, but democracy as
we practise it, with all its defects, is an essential part of the
business of living together in India. We are dissatisfied with the
democratic procedure. We want to improve the democratic procedure, but it is an essential part of our organization, an essential part of our national interest to preserve, or else we will get
into serious political trouble, no matter how advanced the
economic planning or the general advance of the people.

The translation of these national interests, these basic national
interests—and I am going to speak to you this evening of only
these basic issues which do not change—into a policy which safeguards them has to proceed through the evolving, as you know;

of a frame, a framework of thought. The frame provides the contours within which policy is operated. It is the political and economic discipline which must prevail during a given period after internal and external realities have been carefully assessed. The frame changes depending on how these realities change.

All this must sound terribly like the elaboration of a military exercise, but in the political and economic spheres the reality is never so clear as we imagine. Only perceptive leadership can unravel the reality, or, at least, attempt to. We are in every nation speaking of realities, but there are very few elements in these nations who are really attempting to unravel the reality. There is a tendency to accept reality as it is presented by the mass media, and it is in this context that India, I think, was extremely fortunate that the leadership of the non-violent freedom struggle headed by Gandhi, and the eighteen-year-old steward-ship of free India by Nehru, sought to test every policy by the yardstick of continental unity. It was very easy in those days for any type of leadership in India to be carried away by a wave of pressure from the people and to make grave errors, but both Gandhi and Nehru—Gandhi in the conduct of the freedom struggle, and Nehru in the difficult years after freedom—tested every policy on the basis of its impact on every region in India, on every community in India.

The British partition of India was a solid reminder to every Indian of what could happen if he strayed from this path. I believe that this partition was a traumatic experience and made Nehru more conscious than ever before of the need to nurture this unity, particularly in a country which was attempting to develop economically in the political conditions of a free demo-cracy, conditions which usually follow economic development. Democracy could not be abandoned in the interest of speedy economic growth because the sensitive federal character of India, its multi-cultural or multi-national character, made auto-cratic rule impossible. Autocracy could become the excuse for the break-up of federal unity. Indeed, recent events in Pakistan are a significant pointer and a warning!

India was fortunate that Nehru was the first political leader to begin the institutional structuring of the federal political system. He was remarkably sensitive to the complex and ramified reality facing him. Gandhi had given him a perceptive power which others lacked despite their closeness to the Mahatma. To this natural perception, Nehru brought his own rational and scientific disciplines.

The tragic drama of partition had made the leading cadre of the ruling Congress Party obsessive about the unity of India. Nothing was to intrude into political thinking and action which might threaten this unity. The federal character of the State stressed a continental balance of power. Regional elites were boldly recognized and seen as co-sharers in economic growth, commanding regional States of their own. And the interests of the minority communities settled all over the subcontinent were also carefully safeguarded. It was on such foundations that the slogan of democracy, socialism and secularism were coined to provide the framework of national interests.

We undertook the recognition of the linguistic states of India. Despite what partition had done, despite the disorganizations of partition, we went ahead and reorganized linguistically the States of India because of this powerful assertion from the regional elites. The world said Nehru was crazy, but today we realize that this linguistic reorganization, despite all its costs in so many respects keeps India together. This is what gives India political stability despite the wretchedness that is India when you look at it in terms of economic statistics. There is a certain balance, there is a motivation, and this is because there is a response to these federal considerations.

Then the pressure to defend the underprivileged of the many communities of India, particularly those which exist continentally—this is very important—and so strengthen the bonds of federal unity. All minority groups which exist continentally were, in Nehru's mind, the most important element in the building of the unity of the country because the minorities are not regional in character; they are always all-India, and Nehru looked upon them as unifying forces. He looked upon the Muslims in India, 60 million Muslims of India—more than in West Pakistan—as a cementing force if you could win them over. This is an extremely profound observation, in my opinion, of the man's life and work.

Now, these influences he translated into slogans, which are very necessary for the people, particularly a backward developing people. He translated these concepts into slogans so that he could explain them to the people, and explanation in India is done not through the newspaper. It is, as you know, done through public meetings. Millions of people are addressed every month by the political leadership, and it is through these slogans and through these rambling discourses that consciousness develops. Indian leaders are famous as talkers. I think they become talkers because they have to be constantly talking to the people! And in this way, Nehru translated his thinking into the slogans of democracy, socialism and secularism. They met the three points which I earlier elaborated for you, and he repeatedly warned that we could only neglect them at our peril.

Democracy, apart from playing its normal role of political correction and balance, had to be motivated to cement federal unity without frustrating regional aspirations in conditions of underdevelopment. Socialism could not stop short at the build up of public sector activity; it must discipline a proper sharing of resources not only among sections of the people but also among the various differing regions of the subcontinent. This is not easy. And then there was the added complication where you had to, consciously, without saying it, arrange the development of the country in such a way that the various regions of India became dependent on each other. In other words, in the future, our steel plants will be situated in South India and they will draw their raw material from Central India. Normally they should be situated in Central India, but a conscious decision is needed to place them in South India, because it is only then that the states of South India, under tremendous stress at the moment—language agitations, etc.—will understand their linkage to the national market.

This meshing of the economic and political process which we have undertaken and for which we have been severely criticized in the world does some violence to the norms of development. Yes, it is part of nation building.

Secularism demands opposition to any attempt to create what is known as a single-nation State. This should be discouraged firmly, for such an attempt would only undermine a growing federal unity. The Jan Sangh Party in India demands a single-nation image for India, a single language, etc., and this has to be fought constantly by what you might call the Gandhians and Nehruites who stand for a different national personality.

The founding fathers of the Republic believed that the consolidation of the newly-won freedom could only take place within
a framework of political consensus. Confrontations were luxuries to be avoided for the moment. The extraordinary fact has
to be acknowledged that despite underdeveloped conditions the
consensus spirit took root—and even among the revolutionary
parties! The objective of this strategy was only one—to consolidate the frail unity of the subcontinent. I stress this concept of
unity because I think that Indian policy and the confusions that
exist in India will have to be studied by the relation of policy to
the unity of the federal State.

As you know, the national consensus was projected internationally when India gathered her strength in freedom. She had
very little industrial muscle or economic presence, but she was
entering an era which was already nuclear. If she was to combine in her society the humanistic liberal thought of the west
and the egalitarian anti-imperialist ideology of the communist-
socialist world, she would have to project this understanding in
her foreign policy. Non-alignment was a natural, purposeful
answer to the challenge of a world divided dangerously into
blocs. Nehru realized that commitment either way would sharpen
the existing polarization in the world and damage the consensus
within India. This is an extremely important element which has
never been stressed, and explains why so many have called him
"an interferer." The position is that the non-aligned policy of
India rose and was rooted in the Indian consensus, and if he
pursued any other policy he would have wrecked the consensus
internally and damaged the stability of India, and probably
cracked the unity of India forever.

One of Nehru's greatest contributions to this policy was that
he inculcated in the Indian, and built creatively on the Indian
mind, the concept that India, even though it spoke up for certain
principles in the world, would not play a role abroad which
would be tantamount to a physical presence. It would be a voice
for sanity, for principles, part of a mounting international chorus.
India, despite temptations, really does not take a position of
big brother or powerful vengeance-seeker. It confines its physical role to its own borders and works towards a lessening of
whatever we call them, tensions or alignments, which damage
the peace in its area and in the surrounding areas. Indians tend

not to see things in black and white. We have always looked at matters in shades of grey. It is something which I think Hinduism has implanted deeply on the mind of India; whether you are a Hindu or a Muslim or a Christian or a Parsi, you definitely do not take positions in a black and white manner, as is part of the Christian ethic.

Moral features, however, create anger in situations of power politics. Extremists and sectarians do not relish exposure by philosophers who refuse to face realities. India, still living in a *status quo* situation, growing slowly, with classes and castes intact, was more than ordinarily vulnerable. We know what followed. By 1962, the threat to the frontiers of India had eroded the internal consensus. Defence had become a crippling burden and was polarizing political and economic attitudes. A standing army of a million men was sanctioned. Non-alignment itself was fractured. Confusion and discord had set in to take their toll.

I will not go into that period. You are well aware of it. If you carefully survey the Nehru era, you will find that the 1962 events and what followed was not a repudiation of our understanding of national interests and the need to function through a dynamic national consensus, but a pointer to our failure accurately to assess a changing international situation and the experience— positive and negative—which has characterized our internal development. Politics by consensus demands continuous assessment, continuous renewal—or else we become exponents of a dangerous *status quo* mentality. This drift is precisely what occurred, and I shall attempt to explain how.

Take the internal situation first. National unity in the early formative years dictated a democratic set-up on the basis of a mixed economy. Democracy normally is built on economic surplus which comes from a given level of development. We did not have this surplus, but we were determined that we would raise it by various fiscal measures. We also sought foreign assistance. We knew that there was danger in relying on aid. It could subvert or inhibit national independence. However, we maintained that even as we took foreign aid, we would so plan our economy that the commanding heights would be in the control of the State.

As our economy grew, we failed to keep a rigorous check to see that foreign aid only came in at critical points which we could not develop on our own. The colonial type administration which was inherited from the British was good for politically consolidating the infant federal republic (it possessed excellent men trained in law and order techniques), but this iron frame was thoroughly useless in leading economic development. In addition, it had no commitments to the objectives laid down by Nehru.

A gradual dissolution of priorities took place. At the same time, development gave birth to powerful vested interests. It became more and more difficult to compel a fuller utilization of internal resources because the wealthy and privileged always found loopholes to avoid paying the cost of development.

Then came the military confrontation on the frontiers together with a crippling defence burden of over 1000 crores. It rose from 250 crores to 1000 crores. And this was the resource that only yesterday was helping to build the economy and now is building an army.

The situation demanded a radical reassessment of the frame of action. Coercion would have to be applied to the more affluent sections. Belts would have to be tightened. Changes in the social structure would also have to be instituted. But there was a reluctance to apply the coercion. Nehru had lost courage. Dangerous stagnation was sought to be treated by printing more and more money. Prices began to rise unchecked. At the same time, our dependence on foreign aid, even in non-priority economic sectors, began to manifest itself. The spirit of the nation flagged, and there was no leadership to revive it.

Internationally, we had failed to realize that the blocs were disintegrating, that a China need not be disciplined by the Soviet Union, that a Pakistan need not be controlled by the USA. We had not realized this in India, and despite all the tomes that are written about foreign policy and the mistakes that were made, the basic fact is that India had not realized that China was no longer guided by the Soviet Union, and this was a key to our confusions.

Non-alignment was valid but it needed new dimensions, more meaningful cooperation among the non-aligned, greater and more skilful flexibility. When these realizations dawned on us, the internal situation had already become so unhealthy that it was not possible to order a speedy correction. We are today in the process of extricating ourselves from these failures, and it is going to be a difficult process because we have reacted belatedly. Nevertheless, the process will again be disciplined by the concept of a national consensus. There is no other way for federal India. It is slow and costly, but it is the only way. What would be then, the broad outlines of a new national consensus which serves our vital interests? Let me try to sketch it. It is always a hazardous game, and I am only going to sketch that part of it which remains unalterable.

The basic situation in the world, as we see it, is that the two blocs of hostile powers are being replaced by two super powers. There is now general recognition among analysts and observers in India that this situation must be confronted. A disintegration of the blocs has taken place despite the polarizing influence of the Vietnam War and the Czechoslovak happenings. In fact, today we do not know who is aligned and who is non-aligned. Everybody seems to be non-aligned. There will be many upsets in alignments. The non-aligned, including a number of middle states, must act within the flexibility offered by the two super powers. They will find that this flexibility increases as they build wider, multi-lateral contacts to retain their initiatives for peace and progress which are so important to them.

Here again, the frames by which we have lived all these years will have to be reassessed. We have to create new frames within our system of middle states. If we continue to live by the frames by which we have been living so far, we will not move out of this situation. Polycentric development, or the gradual growth of many centres of power, has to be related to the future of non-aligned action. The sectarians in the dying blocs would still like to preserve the old type polarization. Their success would only mean, we believe, that Asia and Africa would be turned into a kind of war zone. In other words, old-type responses will prove sterile. This search for a meaningful understanding of the world situation will be one of the major headaches for not only the developing countries, but also developed nations not anxious to play a servile role to the super powers.

National defence—the second point—has become for us in India a major problem. Viable settlements of border problems will have to be sought, and I think there is a national consensus today on this. We developing nations cannot bear an economically destructive defence burden. At the same time, defence spending in a country with a sprawling land frontier like India's has got to become growth-oriented. This problem has yet to be solved because growth orientation can take place in a highly developed society, but in a developing society growth orientation for defence is extremely difficult.

This would impact defence organization, placing the emphasis on a cheaper, perhaps an equally effective, defence system. All manner of investigation proceeds into this. At the same time, we would have to raise the question of utilizing India's now considerable ordnance capacity to the maximum by collaboration with other non-aligned countries and neighbours. In peace time, only some 25 per cent of the ordnance capacity, which has been built up at considerable cost, is in use, and it is an expensive luxury. If every developing country in South-East Asia is going to build ordnance capacity, I think we are all going to topple our economies! Hence, even military equations might be sought with our non-aligned friends—a personal view of mine!

Somehow, dependence on the super powers has got to be reduced, or else we will find ourselves increasingly inhibited and manipulated within a nuclear argument. This will raise the question also of whether India goes nuclear. It is a ramified question and needs to be answered within the context not of our ability to make the bomb, but our ability to face the cost, economic and political, and there is a very serious political cost.

One of the reasons why I have sketched very clearly the whole structure of Indian unity and the sensitive federal character of the country is to bring it down ultimately to the political implications of an India going nuclear. When you relate the two you realize how grave is the contradiction between the assertion of a military presence and the federal character which does not really give you the motivation to raise the resources for a full nuclear programme. However, I am convinced that we shall be disciplined in the foreseeable future by the overwhelming sentiment of our people to confine themselves to their own borders. This is one of Nehru's great legacies.

Thirdly, internally, we will have to seek greater political cohesion. There are various ways of doing this, but at the root of it all lies the still unresolved business of becoming self-reliant.

If foreign aid is carefully analyzed—or, for that matter, foreign capital investment—it will be found that whereas it is a vital part of the economic surplus which helps to sustain what you might call "the luxury of dissent" in our still developing society, it can become the "grave-digger" of dissent and independence if it leads to subservience instead of self-reliance. It is our job to make aid or foreign investment serve our interests. How? This remains a central question.

Apart from the fact that we have to bargain hard, we have to build equal economic collaboration with a number of smaller nations who have no extra-territorial interests but who are sufficiently advanced to assist us. This field has been totally neglected because it involves harder work, more careful planning and strict implementation of decisions taken. Our lazy system is attracted by the waste which is part of the aiding operation of the super powers, for waste is in a sense the easy profit made by the captains of industry who think of economic growth only in terms of foreign collaboration, foreign know-how and so on. Aid-oriented attitudes will have to be broken in India, and this is one of the tasks to which we are now addressing ourselves. To stop aid altogether at this juncture would dislocate the economy which has unfortunately become aid-dependent. We will have to devise a plan to extricate ourselves from this dependence—and foreign policy helps by opening new contacts which are not inhibiting in the expression of national interests.

And we will have to devise a national consensus which moves our many millioned people. This humanity is, in fact, our greatest wealth, but we have not yet found the way of moving it for constructive tasks and in democracy, without regimentation. This is the central question of the consensus which will determine the future of our country. It could express itself in coalition governments or united fronts. I do believe that the phase of one party rule in India is over.

We may be moving into an extremely complex phase of coalition governments, which are coalitions of the left and coalitions of the right. Within these coalitions we will again have to find points of contact to restructure our federal operation. It is going to be extremely difficult. The system is going to be put to very great strain in the coming years, but it is a phase in our political evolution which we have to go through, and there is a great deal of confidence that we will find the answers.

There should be a final note, that in our developing societies we require one element which is lacking right round the world—an ideology. It has been treated as a bad word in many countries and has come to be regarded as a bad word, but ideology means essentially a dream of the future. There is so much talk about the crisis of man today, but we fail to realize, I feel, that the crisis is rooted in the fact that man for the first time, at the height of his achievement in science and technology, is without a dream. It is this dream, I think, which has to be structured. Otherwise, we are in serious trouble.

5

Dynamic Centrism*

One of the axioms of political development in India is that a dynamic centrist party, capable of forging sanctions for a policy of steady and coordinated economic and social growth, incapacitates the polarizing forces on the Right and Left. Such a party has to be very close to the people, free of rigid and preconceived notions, wedded to honest democratic, secularist and egalitarian objectives, determinedly sovereign in its arduous quest for a socialist order, and always sensitive to the many pulls and pressures of transition in a complex federal system. The Congress Party was able to rule for so long in India because it sought to play this dynamic centrist role. However, deviations invariably placed the party at the mercy of a predatory Right and Left. And this is what is happening now.

Today, the party faces one of the gravest crises of its long and eventful history. During the years of freedom, and particularly in the course of the last decade, the objectives of the party were subverted by lobbies of businessmen, politicians, publicists and the like. Foreign powers also dabbled in this lobbying. As a result, the "commanding heights" are now in the control of men accustomed to serving the objectives of powerful vested interests. The "public sector" has been reduced to a vast employment racket for the elite and its hangers-on, managed by careerist bureaucrats who have little management skill and no commitment

*From *Socialist India*, August 1970.

to the objectives of the party. Urban and rural "administration" is a kind of overlordship vitiated by the worst aspects of an hierarchical system. An antiquated system of rules and regulations, of theoretical accountability, the result of mechanical accretions from planned or free enterprise societies, blocks performance at all levels and is stirred into lazy action only by the nudgings of corruption.

These aspects of the national scene suffocate the massive achievements of the Indian people. A significant industrial capacity has been established in a vast and sprawling subcontinent. Scientific agriculture has taken roots. The industrial revolution coupled with the more complex revolution of science and technology is steadily changing the mores of one of the world's "unchanging" societies. New skills have percolated to the smallest village. New thoughts stir the traditional mind. Centuries of serfdom and oppression are under attack. A new dignity sparks the trust of 550 millions. All this has been achieved in democracy, a slow and expensive process for a developing land.

Against this continental background of change, the parties of the Right and Left are foraging for support. They raise political and economic issues which either have not been resolved or have become more tangled through neglect. The issues, as raised by the Right and Left, are contradictory and confuse large sections of the people who cannot easily separate truth from nonsense. Significantly, the confusion and frustration have been fanned by both Right and Left to violent anger. The militance of the *senas* and *sanghs* of various description on the Right and the violence of the Naxalites and other groups on the Left represent a serious attempt to drown the politics of dynamic centrism, even as efforts are made to revive the *elan* of the Congress Party.

The gravity of the situation facing the ruling party at the centre is underlined by the unthinking activity—or otherwise! —of certain of its own factions, of a right-wing and left-wing character, to involve the party in a strategic and tactical line which would lead inevitably to the politics of polarization as against the politics of dynamic centrism. Swearing by Gandhi and Nehru, both factions work to destroy the wisdom of the founding fathers of the party and to push the leadership in one or the other direction. The attempt over the past few years to neutralize this disruptive and adventurist lobbying within the party by manipulating the play and impact of personalities has been costly, and if it continues it will be fatal to the long-term perspective of national consolidation. Institutional and programmatic answers must be sought if the democratic, federal structure is to be strengthened through the politics of dynamic centrism.

It is tragic that so many of the leading elements of the ruling Congress Party show little understanding of how vital the politics of dynamic centrism are to the future coherence and progress of continental India. Nor do these elements attempt to thrash out the essential content of the politics of dynamic centrism. The disarray of both levels conveys an impression that the politics of dynamic centrism are merely a cover for opportunism and a surrender to vested interests. This impression demoralizes hitherto articulate sections of healthy opinion and creates the opening for the rampages of the parties of the Right and Left.

At a time when the States of continental India are experimenting with coalition governments of the Right and Left, and also with consolidations of a specifically regional character, it seems politically naive to speak of "grand alliances" of the Right or Left at the national level. Such a development would put our federal policy under dangerous strain. Centrism at the Centre, always difficult to sustain because of the many options inherent in centrist postures, helps to avoid confrontation with the federating states. A markedly Left or Right government at the Centre would invite political collisions. Indeed, the threat to the unity of the subcontinent would then be on the agenda. This recognition of reality is slowly impacting political thought, but the intellectual understanding of this highly involved political process needs to be intensified. The warning lessons of history, which tell of centrists aiding polarization by non-action, must be digested. The politics of dynamic centrism must develop a unifying content which inspires the many millions of India, a revolutionary content which cannot become a cover for opportunists of various hues and for the supporters of the present *status quo* of profit and privilege.

Many attempts have been made to define this content. Indeed, no significant idea has escaped the attention of those agitating for such a definition. However, interestingly enough, no one has taken the trouble to evolve a programme which embodies both the solid egalitarian call of the Left and the competitive efficiency in performance which is proclaimed by the Right as broad disciplines. These apparently contradictory positions must be fused for effective action. Invariably, the demand is either for an adventurist, populist left-ward swing or for a cynical pragmatism which enshrines an unhealthy *status quo*. Until the most effective amalgam of so-called Right and Left policies is put together in the interest of economic growth, there is constant danger of the concept of dynamic centrism being washed away in spreading anger, frustration and violence.

In other words, new values must be uncovered to crystallize new priorities. Dynamic centrism must become a revolutionary doctrine which challenges the dead slogans of the Right and the Left. The growth models of planned and free enterprise societies are beginning to look very similar, particularly in their dedication to consumption-orientation. Perceptive thinkers would cry halt to the drive for wasteful living, the hunt for more and more of what one does not need. India's many millions cannot hope to prosper on the basis of such models. New paths to mass prosperity must be found. Employment, food, housing and transport must be tackled in a totally new way. The old remedies have failed. They were based on value systems which are no longer relevant. Economic, political and the social thinking must be mobilized for a massive attack on poverty. This revolution of integrity must be the core of dynamic centrism. Only then will the base of our continental society stabilize. And there is no time to be lost.

Only when the strategic and tactical line of the ruling Congress Party is spelled out, will it be possible for the other parties to detail their positions. The present-day confusion in our politics is caused directly by the play of personalities which has replaced the confrontation of ideas, policies and programmes. It is the paramount duty of the political activists of the ruling Congress Party to compel their leaders to face the programmatic challenge. In this, they will enjoy the full support of not only the mass of our people but also of our intellectual and specialist opinion.

6

Emerging Pattern of Politics and Leadership*

Emerging patterns . . . . What are these emerging patterns? As
far as I can see, two patterns are visible. With the breakdown
of the all-embracing, amorphous Congress Party—the formation
which led our people to freedom—we see, in the first place, the
emergence of multi-party coalitions, fronts, ("united" and
"democratic"), *dals* of various descriptions and militant parochial regional parties. Secondly, as a response to the splintering
of various parties and consolidations, there is developing an
urge, particularly at the central level, to rally around a leader
or group of leaders. It is believed, and fairly widely, that such
a development would impart a degree of stability to an uncertain, transitory situation. The Central authority would be
strengthened, and political-economic perspectives restored.

A great deal of political education has taken place as a result
of the experiences of the last few years. Coalitions lacking
commitment to a programme are of a temporary nature, and
this inevitably places greater and greater power in the hands of
the permanent civil service which provides the only continuum
in a fluid situation. Government by minority, as at the Centre,
is possible, given the necessary political skill, but it tends to

*A talk delivered at the National Defence College, New Delhi,
January 1969.

place the ruling party in a position where it can be pressurized, even blackmailed. Small wonder, then, is the demand for coalitions based on agreed programmes, as also the equally persistent and parallel search to find a ruling party with a clear majority.

We should not be disturbed by these broad developments. They are part of the business of political growth. The great formation of the freedom struggle, the Indian National Congress, an unifying platform for diverse trends, has passed through the phase of its continental overlordship. Political growth takes its toll of unity. New formations arise. New alignments are tested. Even polarizations are sought. There is a great ferment taking place in India today which is bound to throw up new consolidations. The next phase could be marked by a multiplicity of coalitions in the States committed to precise programmes and a similar development at the Centre. To begin with, these coalitions would be unstable. Partners in power have to learn to live as partners in power. It's a healthy discipline, but it takes some time to develop. Then again, with the separation of Central and State elections and a possible bolder thrust by the ruling Congress Party, we may yet be spared coalitions at the Centre. The democratic experience of 25 years cannot really be dissolved merely because problems of various kinds have arisen.

Everyone, in a sense, is an authority on emerging patterns of politics and leadership. We cannot help ourselves, because in one way or another this activity intrudes into our lives. We develop many fixed attitudes—some of them, pretty dogmatic, and conditioned by background, education and economic interest! But because we are all experts in a major or minor sense, immense problems are created in evolving a common understanding of the factors which impact the growth of our parties in democracy. A thousand different and contrary analyses are available to confuse and paralyze our thought. I am going to try and cut through the jungle of theories in an attempt to find some broad guiding principles.

Party politics and parliamentary democracy do not live in a vacuum. In India, the political scientist's view is congested by all manner of considerations which are, in several ways, unique to parties in a democracy. Let me list the peculiarities, to begin with:

(*a*) The country is vast and sprawling. It is developing, not underdeveloped. Communications are not primitive. The population is huge, and growing furiously.

(*b*) The contrasts in the land are equally impressive. Poor and rich. Majorities and minorities. The backward and the advanced. Mountain and plain. Delta and desert. Everything you can imagine. The shadow of a partition is ever present. Continental unity is of recent vintage. The unity obsession is very real.

(*c*) India is not a single-nation State. It is a federal complex of many communities with highly developed cultures and aspirations. Animosities too!

(*d*) Here, class is not the only base and lever of political activity. Caste and community impinge heavily to influence commitment and motivation. Overlapping loyalties are a special feature. Classic confrontations are blurred.

(*e*) There is the massive nature of the economic, social and cultural problems which compels an involvement in continuing policies. These policies, though receiving different emphases, are wedded to the concept of broad egalitarianism—and the resulting radicalism which it engenders.

These major peculiarities of the Indian situation are not unique individually, but as an amalgam they present a unique situation. Indian politics cannot be projected, analyzed and understood if we take a mechanical view which is conditioned by western theory and precept. Nor can Marxian dogma be applied. Both these tools are useful, but more integral attitudes are needed to understand the Indian political reality. I do not want to sound pompous or chauvinistic, but we are in fact dealing with continental politics—and I don't believe that this kind of challenge presents itself anywhere else in the world—no, not even in the USA or the USSR where situations are very different.

The logic of continental politics in India has to be studied if we are to understand the special qualities of political parties in our country and the functioning of parliamentary democracy. In other words, we have to see how the peculiarities which I have sketched roughly affect political expression and development. Again, I shall not go into obvious details, but confine myself to the more significant characteristics which provide the fascinating facets to Indian political science:

First, in the interest of unity, the need for a responsive, continental balance of power and opportunity dictates the very sensitive federal character of our State—so sensitive, indeed, that it is often mistaken as a weak and fragile structure. There has been no parallel. It is like putting Europe, East and West, under a single government.

Second, the powerful, persistent assertion of the regional elites and the specialized interests of caste and community dictate a continental sharing of economic resources. Pure economic considerations cannot be the sole yardstick in national development. There is a constant interplay of politics and economics—much more so than in single nation States. All concepts—like planned growth and free enterprise—must be understood in this special context or else we will be talking in the air. Mechanical application of western experience is untenable.

Third, there is a continental and unifying pressure to defend the interests of the less fortunate—a brotherhood of "have-nots"—and, similarly, through secular safeguards the essential interests of the many and sizeable communities inhabiting the subcontinent, particularly those which exist continentally and strengthen the bonds of federal unity.

Fourth, and for the same federal reasons, a constant search goes on for leadership which cements continental unity. The Indian political mind functions at two levels—at the level of community and at the level of nation. Different tests are applied for different levels of leadership. Increasingly, this quest places significant power in the hands of a tiny, modernizing elite, trained in western ways and capable of functioning in a language like English which cuts across internal boundaries of regions, castes and communities. It is not a healthy situation and creates tensions and complications of a kind not experienced by single-nation States.

Before I go further, let me apply some of these ideas to the growth of political parties in our country. If our political parties are like those in any other country, then what I am saying is so

much stuff and nonsense. If not, then I think some solid thinking must be done on the conditioning influences. The trouble
with elite politics, particularly of an elite heavily influenced by
the English language, is that it tends unthinkingly to apply
Anglo-Saxon notions to the reality around—in fact, distorts the
reality to fit the notions. It is my conviction that a great deal of
the cynicism and demoralization in the Indian elite today is
rooted unconsciously in its inability to understand India in
Indian terms.

But let us leave that for the moment. Let me try and sketch
some of the influences bearing heavily on the political growth of
our parties:

(*a*) Region, caste and community interests are forcing
parties, particularly those witnessing rapid growth today in
certain restricted areas, to reflect a narrow, parochial understanding.

(*b*) The passing of leaders who enjoyed continental acclaim,
because of their role in the freedom struggle, and the absence
of such continental personalities in the new leadership, tends
to strengthen regionalism.

(*c*) Parties which are being pushed by events to seek continental status find themselves compelled to revise political
theory and programme in order to make it relevant continentally. This creates confusion among the cadres in the
strong-holds—cadres not concerned with party expansion.
Factions and splits are the order of the day.

(*d*) The search for an all-India continental status and relevance blunts ideological sharpness between the parties. The
complexity of problems and the need to arrive at a series of
consensuses between various pressures and pulls, turns even
revolutionaries into exponents of an amorphousness which
they condemned earlier. Our parties could well be likened to
members of an Hindu Undivided Family with a number of
kartas fighting for succession!

(*e*) Broadly, no alternative paths are presented. Democracy
is vital federally to cushion, amend and mould contradictory
demands. Socialism or egalitarianism is vital if a varied
and diverse subcontinent is to develop economic coherence.
Secularism is vital because it is not possible to attempt a

single-nation state in the complexity that is India. The past of the continent holds many warnings. Decentralization is a vital major trend. The enormity of India indicates this.

(*f*) In other words, traditional revolutions are not possible in India, nor coups, civil and military. Such activity would shatter federal unity—and is indulged in only by isolated groups not interested in unity.

(*g*) There is a running battle in every party between the consensus-makers and the polarizers. It spills over party divisions, creates changing alignments and realignments of a surprising kind. But consensus-making remains a dominant and decisive trend. A total confrontation between political Right and political Left is sought to be blunted.

I believe very firmly that the politics of consensus cannot be side-tracked in India. These politics will continue to have a profound impact. Of course, the new peasant elites, now moving into the legislatures, lack the sophistication of the earlier elites and tend to express themselves rather crudely and forcefully, but here too the processes of modernization will rapidly transform the scene. However, we must recognize that in today's situation three models of political action are in fierce competition:

(*i*) The Coalitionists wedded to status-quoism and slow change.

(*ii*) The Centrists pledged to a mixed economy and dynamic democratic change.

(*iii*) The Leftists seeking progress through active polarization.

Each model has its own contradictions. The Coalitionists cannot survive in status-quoism. The Centrists find their dynamics not adequately revolutionary. The Leftists know that polarization is only meaningful if it occurs continentally or else it leads to the destruction of national unity.

In this kind of situation, the ruling Congress Party holds many of the aces. By and large, it is the inheritor of the traditions of the freedom movement. It commands a continental organization. And, programmatically, it has the potential to be

flexible and to find the strategy and tactics which would motivate the many millions of India in town and village. It is paralyzed only because the party tends to fight in its traditional
manner, between its left, right and centrist factions. The moment
this fight is ended by an unifying and revolutionary consensus,
in a meaningful policy and programme, the other parties organized behind other models are compelled to expend themselves
in reacting, not leading. This is the basic reality in India today.
The Centrists lead, but are unable to formulate their revolutionary, motivating doctrine.

It may rightly be asked what such a doctrine could be.
Naturally, it has to avoid the pitfalls of rightist and leftist
slogan-mongering—and yet achieve a positive synthesis of what
is best in the credo of the rightist and leftist orientations. I believe that increasingly the Centrists, whether in coalition or
under the hegemony of a single party, will move towards a mass
line. Such a mass line would cut across the common ideological
barriers and focus on the key problems facing the people.

    (*i*) The high cost of necessities for mass consumption;
    (*ii*) The terrible lack of jobs or mass employment;
    (*iii*) The deplorable absence of mass housing and transport:
    (*iv*) The deteriorating situation in mass health;
    (*v*) The confusions in the drive for mass literacy.

These critical areas of mass concern bristle with problems which
can only be effectively tackled if we radically alter the antiquated administrational system by which we function. Our refusal
to attack the system can therefore put a big question mark over
the entire structure of present-day society. Problems at the mass
level cannot be tackled with old, rusty weapons belonging to
another age.

In this connection, I would like to mention that the elaboration of a mass line will demand a shaking up of our priorities.
Necessities before luxuries. Jobs in the shape of land armies.
Mass housing before individual homes. Mass transport before
the private car. Effective mass literacy and continuing education
before the cult of pointless university degrees. This is not as
easy as it sounds. Large sections of influential people will oppose
policies which effect their standards of living. They would want

to continue to be the flies on the dung heap. But men and movements do not wait on events. They create them. Good leadership keeps abreast of events, even ahead of them. The Centrist consensus-makers will have to do just that, or be thrown aside.

If we face failure in this phase of adjustment, I think the peculiar pressures within the continental situation of India will compel political re-thinking in the direction of a presidential system, based upon smaller States and upon Central legislatures which act as sounding boards for a democratically elected Head of State. How a transition will be made from the chaos of coalitions to an ordered presidential system, is in the realm of speculation. Someone with the gumption to address history will probably turn up and carry the mandate of the people. However, there is no threat to democratic functioning, for continental, multi-communal, multi-cultural, multi-national India cannot survive without the tussle and bustle of the open society. Autocratic rule would have a limited tenure—unless, of course, it develops divine overtones!

7

Cleansing the Elections*

India has entered the phase where qualitative changes are required in the structuring of her continental politics. The debate that is now joined ranges over a wide canvas. Should we move towards a presidential system? Would it be politically realistic to break the "one language, one State" formula behind our federal structure and increase the number of States by reorganizing new, independent stirrings within the existing States? Are we too centralized in certain respects and too decentralized in others? And so it goes on, this healthy questioning of the viability of our democratic institutions.

The most fundamental area of discussion is naturally the business of elections. The absence of well-organized all-India parties, the entry of a large number of political operators who seek to exploit the system for their own ends, the distortion manifest in results between votes polled and seats won, the growing misuse of political power, the parallel breakdown of the norms of democratic functioning in various subtle ways, and, above all, the terrible cost of elections to individual candidates and contesting parties has brought the focus on to the question of clean elections.

Why "clean?" Because the very cost—apart from other social factors—sparks massive corruption. The adoption by use of the British system of elections without regard to the complexities of

*From *Seminar* 159, November 1972.

India's continental politics has placed us in a predicament. In high moral fervour, unable to organize party funds by mass collections, we also legislated against company "donations" which it was alleged, favoured the parties of the present exploitative *status quo*. This reform has sanctified corruption on a colossal scale. Industrial tycoons, businessmen and smugglers of various description now contribute "in black money" to party funds "individually"—and, of course, expect appropriate rewards.

The disaster inherent in this situation is at last becoming apparent to us. It is clear that if we do not wish to crack the very bases of our democratic functioning, we will have to agree at the level of an overwhelming majority of parties to take certain fundamental remedial measures, possibly before the next general elections. This is not at all impossible. Those who speak for the *status quo* are either timid about change or are not honest in their intentions about the functioning of a healthy and creative democratic life for India's continental system. In other words, the reform must begin.

It is not my intention to go into a long argumentation over the kind of suggestions that have been advanced by various quarters. I will confine myself to an area of discussion where a kind of consensus is developing between the parties of the so-called Right and Left. I refer to the growing propagation of the system of proportional representation as the most effective answer available at the moment to some of the ills of the present system.

Traditionally, proportional representation is described as a system which leads to a multiplicity of parties and coalition politics which are highly unstable—and likely to be even more so in the caste-influenced, plural society that is federal India. The criticism, largely from Anglo-Saxon sources, can be met by advancing the example of a country like the German Federal Republic which practises the system of proportional representation but cancels out all parties unable to score a certain percentage of the total vote. We could do likewise in India. And, there are important lessons to be learned from neighbouring Ceylon.

Proportional representation, as a system, is also seen as something which divorces the tribunes of the people from their constituencies and given encouragement to "bosses" in the organization. There is a certain validity in this assessment, but then no system can be described as perfect—or, for that matter, made perfect. Indeed, even today in India, the politician is cynical about his constituents and we have vivid examples from the past and the present of "bossism."

It is important that we should, by trial and error, move towards a more scientific democratic expression in our society. The individualistic striving at the core of the present system of elections is not in keeping with the spirit of our times. It breeds operators who are corrupt, and in a sense, acclaimed for precisely this reason in what has become the murky area of politics.

We have to realize that in this age of traumatic change, the political party as a vital institution has to be strengthened. It alone possesses the capacity to articulate the needs of a section of the people and to work for their fulfilment. A multiplicity of parties represents a multiplicity of sections. This is the confrontation which sparks change. To ensure the process against anarchy, political splinters will have to struggle more energetically or face extinction in the legislatures.

Proportional representation compels political parties to present coherent programmes, to lay the stress on issues rather than personalities, and provides the facility to nominate, on the basis of the votes polled, men and women who understand their job as legislators. The illiterate politician is no longer an inevitability. The complexity of modern life with its demand for many skills and specializations, can be reflected in the legislatures. Indeed, politics is removed from the clutches of the unprincipled operators, the cynical fixers and the openly corrupt. It becomes a task, both imperative and compelling, for the finest minds in the social system.

Apart from these obvious benefits, let us test the proportional representation system with the challenge of "cleanliness," if it may be so called. Under this new system, it would be possible drastically to reduce the amount of money that goes into the holding of an election. Let me try and list some of the obvious packages of reforms which could be introduced under proportional representation and which is impossible under the present system.

(*i*) Election funds would be established under an enlarged Election Commission at Central and State level to publicize the responsibilities of citizens in an election year, to print the appeals of all the political parties, to cover the area of the election without discrimination, and to print all the other materials which assist voters to cast their ballot, including lists of candidates to be nominated by the parties should they get the required number of votes.

(*ii*) It would be the responsibility of the Election Commission working though all-party committees to check voters lists and to update them methodically, a continuing process which is subject to much abuse when the responsibility rests only with citizens and with parties.

(*iii*) In the context of the massive expansion of radio and television in the coming years, it would be the permanent task of the Election Commission to ensure saturation coverage for the parties in these State-controlled media, and, of course, to see that the mass media are not misused by the ruling party at the Centre and in the States.

These three tasks, fundamental to the election process, would cover all those areas which are serviced by corruption money, money which vitiates the moral fibre of the party that comes to power. Taken over by the Election Commission, in the manner suggested, these tasks would be disciplined to that extent.

The Election Commission would have to be suitably reorganized, expanded and insulated against pressures of all kinds. This can be done if there is a will to do it. As for the cost of the scheme, it would be less wasteful and destructive than the acceptance of the *status quo*.

If the political parties of India could be persuaded to begin the exploration, theoretical and practical, of this reform in specifically Indian conditions, it would be necessary to establish certain norms as to their own functioning during the critical electioneering period. Money can corrupt at the level of agitation, demonstration, mass meetings and what have you. Vast funds can be expended on this sort of populism. Obviously, a healthy, meaningful political system has to push electioneering into a person-to-person, house-to-house approach—at least for several weeks before the casting of the vote.

When dealing with a population of 550 million, which is likely to expand in the next 25 years into anything between 800 to 1000 million, we can no longer live at peace with the democratic practices we have so far adopted. They must be constantly reviewed, tested, adjusted, refashioned, altered and modified in order to motivate and discipline the democratic processes. Failure to do this creates the anarchist urges with which we are again becoming familiar. So, very often, anarchism is merely the harbinger of fascism.

Obviously, at the guts of this short plea for urgent reforms in our democratic functioning, lies the future role of the Election Commission. It cannot remain the inadequate instrument that it is today. It must become a major weapon of the reform. This needs early recognition where power rests. The next lot of elections are not so far away.

8

Conformism*

Whenever I consider the problem of censorship in India, and
this is a frequent consideration for any writer in our couutry, I
cannot help but refer to the related problem of conformism.
Censorship and conformism go hand in hand, one feeding and
battening on the other. The invisible force which links them
is fear, fear of the non-conformist on the part of the censor,
fear of the censor and those who stand behind him on the part
of the conformist. Both the conformist and the censor attempt
to envelop their fears with a "philosophy" which is made up of
political, economic or sociological argumentation. But remove
the "dressing," and fear in all its guises is exposed. Unless we
recognise this fear for what it is, there can be no effective tackling of the problem of censorship—or, for that matter, of conformism.

The parent who over-protects his child, the suppressed wife
who cannot voice her grievances, the office worker who never
gets the opportunity to exercise any responsibility, the execu-
tive who believes in obeying mechanically the orders received
"from the top," the professional who has not known the satisfaction of being brutally frank, the writer, painter and artists
who play it safe are all the victims of various degrees of fear,
of censorship, of conformism. An entangling and complex "system" of pressures is at play in both democratic and authorita-

* From *Seminar* 47, July 1963.

rian societies to deepen the control of the ruling elites. Only the confirmed anarchist can see the system in its awful rawness. As for the rest, they campaign against this or that pressure in the hope that these individual battles will one day break the system and create the basis for building a healthy respect for dissent, for non-conformism. The extent to which this campaign against the system is conducted is a reflection of the maturity of a family, a community, a nation. And this applies to capitalist or socialist societies, despite the talk about "priorities" and such things.

India is a most pertinent example of the system at work: a traditionalist society, with all the deeply ingrained inhibitions of paternalism, feudalism, caste and bureaucracy, caught in a network of laws and regulations left behind by the British who ruled absolutely and did not tolerate organized dissent despite liberal pretensions, India came under the administrative sway of men whose purpose was somehow to condition the thinking of the "illiterate masses" and to blunt the radical dreams of "foreign-oriented" intellectuals. In whichever direction you turn today in India you see an extraordinary degree of conformism achieved by the most sophisticated methods. It will be argued that the system, or whatever you call it, exists in most countries and in many it has failed to bend the back of the non-conformist, the dissenter, the oppositionist, the seeker after new truths, the restless, soaring spirit. Then how was it able to crush in so short a period after the struggle for freedom the stirrings of a new India?

Several factors contributed to the collapse: general economic backwardness; lack of opportunity to pursue independent vocations; the early acceptance of the need to link with a powerful Establishment in order to survive; the close control exercised by a small elite over the levers of political power whether at the Right or the Left or the Centre; the rapid projection and consolidation of caste and community interests together with their general acceptance as being necessary to the working of "democracy"; and the equally urgent task to "integrate" the country by giving each region "a stake" in the future. These "realities" were real enough. They served to dissolve the dreams of pre-Independence days and the stuff of which they were made. Very soon, the small elite which had taken over from the British

overlords was itself frightened by the prospect of becoming isolated among the teeming millions. Being sophisticated, anxious
to preserve the democratic trappings, it decided to rob these
teeming millions of their potential leaders by building an elaborate and ramified structure of patronage in the towns and in the
villages.

This approach received the unthinking approval of the would-
be dissenters, of the creative workers and dreamers. Unacquaint-
ed with the habit of democracy, immature in the new experience of patronage, they welcomed the steps that were to follow.
They could not see that their participation would finally maim
their own capacities, would carry them on a wave of values over
which they would have no control. Supposedly democratic institutions and organizations sprang up to cater to various strata of
intellectuals and workers in the creative arts. These were heavily
subsidized, officially blessed, and quite clearly necessary for what
is known as "official recognition." Over the years, they have
smothered criticism of any kind in public—even in the vital fields
of economic, political and social research! Ironically enough,
there is a substance in the charge that India is much the poorer
for the lack of angry young men. And in this process of pulveris-
ing independent probing thought, foreign foundations have played their part offering recognition and reward only to those
scholars who are "safe" and "useful."

But the system in India did not stop at buying off the intellectuals and creative workers. The educated mass and the traditional leaders of society drawn from the more well-to-do sections
of both urban and rural society have been absorbed in movements assuming pompous names such as the National Discipline
Scheme and Bharat Sewak Samaj. Even the Sadhus have their
Samaj! The Gandhians, too. Together with the Home Guards,
the Territorials, the N.C.C., and the A.A.C., the "mass movements" are controlled by an all-pervasive patronage. The disease
which makes India increasingly soft, apathetic, purposeless,
slow-moving and, therefore, superficially mature and temperate
in comparison to neighbouring regions—is rooted in this system
of patronage. Only the economically independent can afford
the luxury of non-conformism, and even they are few and far
between.

The system has paid silent dividends, but the founding fathers are beginning to realize that it has its own laws of growth. They are worried by its capacity to absorb an increasing quantity of funds and resources without tangible return. They do not relish the advice they receive from interested quarters to the effect that the "institutionalization" of patronage, or corruption, is necessary for the continuance of a "stable" democracy; although it is clear that reluctance to nurture the system will excite not only those who have been patronized and pampered, but make dangerous demagogues of those currently qualifying to be embraced by the system. They also know that the stage is fast approaching when it will not be possible to maintain the present rate of growth of the system, unless the system itself throws up the means and methods to sustain itself—in other words, the mobilization and employment of labour power. And of this there is no evidence.

As the contradiction between the mounting investment in patronage and its inability to silence dissent sharpens, the use of censorship powers will become more and more open. In India, we are now entering this phase. The challenges spawned by the threat to our frontiers, the increasing outlay on defence and the heavy taxation are already making influential policy-making circles critical of the waste involved in maintaining the system, or what is recognized as the structure of patronage. When the political parties single out individual targets for attack, the ruling elite will be compelled to retreat. Then, the resort to censorship, open threats and crude pressures to make people conform, will become part of our everyday life. In fact, the first indications of this development are already visible to those who observe the passing scene in the States of the Indian Union. The immense power wielded by Chief Ministers, the easy resort to strong man tactics the moment these powers are challenged, the use by the party machine of bribery and graft, open and subtle, to silence the critical, and the growing conviction among the oppositionists within and without the ruling party that they too must use these stratagems to survive, are prominent aspects of the maturing crisis.

The easy and frequent assumption of special powers at any and every opportunity at both Union and State levels has also numbed the sensitivities of those who would otherwise protest against these violations of democratic and civilized behaviour;

the ruling elite and those who serve it have similarly been corrupted by the exercise of autocratic powers. The invisible force of fear, which inevitably links censorship and conformism, will become more visible as these processes reach their fulfilment.

In this kind of situation, how are we to develop the muscle to oppose the system? Simultaneous activity on two fronts is needed. First, it is necessary to enshrine respect for the non-conformist at every level of our national life and a corresponding contempt for those who conform in fear. Second, organized vigilance is the only answer to the activities of the autocrat who has to be made to understand that no liberty will be surrendered without a fight. These two aspects of the battle for the survival of the democratic and civilized life have been sadly neglected even by those who make noises about defending the right to dissent.

Obviously, the effort to develop respect for the non-conformist should take priority over the effort to create sanctions against those who would violate our liberties. Only when we have demolished the closed-in attitudes, before which reason is swept away, can we hope to mount a movement for fundamental liberties. In other words, a free mind has to be cultivated. This is no easy task. To sift the truth from the maze of contradictory trends is a long and continuous process—and the minds of young and old have to be re-equipped for this confrontation. The young must be salvaged from the deadening grip of conformism. And they can be. In classroom and on the playfields, through their teachers and textbooks, fearlessness to express their thoughts and feelings must be encouraged. It must become the essential ingredient of character building. Similarly, the safe and easy, follow-the-herd attitude must be deplored, rooted out. Only then can we save our children from becoming the future victims of mass hysteria, revivalism or what have you.

But what of the old who continuously influence the young ones and among whom conformism has taken root? In our backward, paternalistic societies the old must also be converted, or the battle will remain uneven and the final result uncertain.

A start should be made through the active propagation of the reasons for establishing respect for the differences we see in others. Carefully it will be argued that it is the conformist mind which is the breeding ground of hatred and violence, a mind which sometimes actively works towards revivalist notions as a defence against the currents of new thought and assumes fascistic postures. It will also become clear that through the wider acceptance of the non-conformist mind, the free mind, an easing of communications takes place between one mind and another. This is vital. Communication becomes real only when it reflects genuine expression and it can only be genuine when it is fearless and it can only be fearless in today's fast-transforming world when it is non-conformist.

Through these realizations, the demand will form possibly even among the old, that man's mind must seek the fresh air, the contest of ideas, the fire of debate—as did the minds of those remarkable men and women who have influenced the thought and endeavour of us earthlings through the centuries. For, non-conformism has always been the great catalyst of change. Even as the mood is created to defend the dissenter, to study his views, to put accepted truths to the test, to loosen the grip of the conformists, it will be necessary to produce the organizational channels through which this mood is able to express itself in support of the free mind and against those "techniques," subtle or otherwise, which seek to smother it. Only then will we be able to make an impact on the summits of power. In this respect, we have done practically nothing.

There was a time in India when the movement for civil liberties cut across party labels and carried the sanction of millions. But no longer. The "techniques" of the party in power have had effect—temporarily, we hope. For, somehow, we must work towards a society in which men are mature enough to be their own censors.

9

Perspectives on the Press*

Some of us who had a ring-side seat during the height of the Chinese invasion could not help remarking on the tragic failure of the Press to confront the challenges posed by this unexpectedly alarming experience. Of course, it is easy to find comforting explanations for the parochial behaviour of our Press, its easy submission to the pressures of the moment, its appetite for an opportunistic political play, its lack of sustained convictions and its shallow pontificating on any and every issue. During these recent, tense weeks, the exceptions were few. In a sense, the Press reflected the unhealthy state of our polity. All the more reason that some attempt be made to probe deeper into the causes of this steep decline in integrity and standards, and to find remedies.

If there is one point on which most Indian journalists, chair-based or working, agree, it is this: that since Independence the Press has come increasingly under the direct control of the leaders of industry who have relegated it to a position of secondary importance in their sprawling empires. The Press has become a kind of power lever which is used every now and then to wrest business concessions from a government which appears to be all-powerful but is not really so. This subsidiary role shows no signs of changing, despite the growth in newspaper circulations and the conspicuous rise in profits. Actually, profitable

*From *Seminar* 42, February 1963.

publishing has encouraged proprietors and managers to purchase the independence of leading members of the profession, to dissolve what little missionary zeal they had left with them.

The collapse of independent, responsible and sparring journalism is mirrored particularly in the daily newspapers. A sameness prevails. The pattern repeats itself not only in the presentation of news, but in the use of language, photographs and other aids available in these swiftly-changing times. Over the years, monotony has destroyed interest in the editorial columns with the result that efforts are now made to inject views into news in order to make stories more readable. In imitative fashion, we have created a host of special correspondents without realizing their true function within the structure of a newspaper. Every publisher follows his most successful neighbour. Every newspaper looks and talks like the other. And the style approximates to something which existed in the west in the twenties.

The situation is somewhat more encouraging where weeklies and periodicals are concerned, for these have not yet been devoured by the giant publishers. Here, a sense of mission does exist. But expanding literacy will make this field profitable too. Then, the same deadening influence, which has made the daily newspaper impotent, will spread and kill what little experimentation does exist in the world of regular publishing. Again, that fast-disappearing specimen, the independent journalist, will be cornered and pressurized to surrender his right to inform, educate and interpret according to his own understanding.

These trends are not special to India. Only, in an underdeveloped society, they have the effect of enthroning the conformists, subjugating the will of those who would project new ideas and concepts, creating a mental and organizational paralysis which makes it impossible to build a genuinely democratic system of communication. This, then, is the major blockage which has to be removed. Can it be done by merely enunciating the "rights" of working journalists without establishing the sanctions for implementing them? Is it axiomatic that only a roused and vigilant profession can salvage its independence? Or should we begin to think of legislating the liberation of the Press from the control of industrial empires? These are urgent questions if we wish to make the foundations of a democratic State secure.

A subservient Press, beholden to industrial magnates and through them to officialdom, can only spawn subservient journalists. To imagine that such a Press is free and therefore superior to its counterpart in a totalitarian society is the worst kind of self-deception. Such a press creates the impression of independence, but can be made to behave tamely if the interest of the owners so dictate. And even when it does act independently, it does so only to serve the larger and selfish aims of the owners. It could well be argued that a Press of this type demoralizes the defenders of democracy and dissent and gives rise to those very arguments which are advanced to quicken its end. Recent history provides many pointed warnings, and India might well witness a repetition of the experience of other societies which were considered less vulnerable to totalitarian concepts.

Already, the symptoms of the collapse are visible. At a discount are newspapermen with a nose for news; they are described as mischief-mongers, not trouble-shooters. The modern journalistic genius is either an unashamed propagandist of the businessman-proprietor or a colourless individual prepared to write to order. Real journalists do exist, but they have made their peace with the new order, fully conscious that they will spend their professional lives frustrated and embittered. Cynicism grows. There seems no way of escape. If the businessman-proprietor demands conformity, so does the communist collective. How is the satellite press to emerge to independence? How are the working journalists and the potentially fearless editors to be salvaged? Is it possible in the present circumstances to build or sustain a truly independent press?

We cannot put our entire faith in the legislative process. It is slow and susceptible to the influence of powerful lobbies organized precisely by those elements who hold the Press in bondage. Nor can we be over-confident about the possible growth of independent ventures. It is almost impossible in today's inflation-actuated economy for anyone but the business or industrial magnate to think of such a venture. Let alone a daily newspaper, which to survive would require a minimum capital of some Rs. 50 lakhs, even a financially stable and competitive weekly would necessitate a Rs. 10 lakhs project; if less is invested, as is often the case in Indian language newspapers and weeklies, the product is seldom competitive. And men of substance are unlikely to invest in these ventures when stock markets offer better returns. Such is the prospect.

A number of journalists' cooperatives have in the past attempted unsuccessfully to launch independent daily newspapers owned by the readers. Invariably, the projects were under-capitalized and the working group lacked managerial and editorial leadership to cope with printing costs, distribution headaches and advertising problems. Lack of leadership also encouraged factional squabbles within the working group. These cooperative ventures collapsed within months of starting and now there is no appetite for "another day," although efforts are still being made to launch newspaper ventures with adequate independent finance.

Looking at the problem realistically, the conclusion is inescapable that the growth of an independent Press will only take place as the result of successful enterprise in the field of weeklies and journals. Here, big money can be made if circulations are built up. How to get at the readership? While language barriers militate against the concentrated sales of published material, whatever market does exist seems to have been monopolized by those who have over long years built up huge distribution machines. Nevertheless, there is still tremendous scope for enterprising publishers who are prepared to employ the best talent and to utilize the tremendous advances made in the collection and presentation of news. But money must be found to organize the sale of product. No independent and effective distribution network exists.

Ask any new entrant into the publishing field to explain his major hurdle, and he will tell you that the funds required to get a magazine across to the readers, to build up an organization for distribution, is well beyond average capacity. Each independent venture carries the heavy financial burden of an independent distribution set-up, and it is naturally not nearly as effective as working through normal distribution channels which have been developed in western countries. These heavy overheads, and the slow growth of sales which inhibits advertisers, destroy the competitive capacity of the independent ventures and take a heavy toll of their financial reserves. Only a huge investment in promotion can correct the balance, and this investment no one can afford to undertake.

A remedy must be found, a remedy which will create a healthy base for competition between the affluent and non-affluent, which will make it easier to plan and invest in new publishing ventures, which will give the journalist who values his independence the chance to test his mettle against those who sit astride in comfortable saddles today, which will shake the established publishers from their security. From the numerous discussions which have taken place, one interesting and logical suggestion has emerged—that steps should be taken to establish an autonomous, cooperative, countrywide distribution net-work for newspapers and journals on a strictly commercial basis. The details of the structure and the manner in which it is to be administered could easily be worked out, and the State could offer financial backing in the early stages. This is the time to launch such an enterprise, when the nation has been through a frightening experience and strives for expression.

While the provision of a distribution network is the crux of the matter, for it will enable readers to decide what they want to read, some solid thinking also needs to be done on the printing facilities available in the country. Here also, cooperative ventures assisted by the State could increase the competitive strength of independent publishing projects, apart from reducing the capitalization necessary in independent printing presses. The technical base of the Press is too atomized at the moment to ensure quality and efficiency for the independent; small-scale printing shops, working on antiquated machinery and charging maximum rates, are the bane of the independent publisher. Cooperative printing presses, organized on an economic scale, would give the independents that vital edge in the competitive battle.

My desire in stressing the need to reinforce the competitive strength of the independent publisher is based on the feeling that a large number of leading advertisers are none too happy with the Press as it exists. They are conscious that their "displays" are being buried in the advertisement-crowded dailies, that few take note of them, that stereotyped news columns damage the reader's interest in the advertisement columns, that circulations provide no indication as to message-carrying capacity, that it would be good sense to find new media for putting their companies and products across. If this new media were established and able to command interest in definite sections of the community, there is every reason to believe that advertisers would be the first to realize the value of these ventures.

In other words, the profession has to develop new perspectives about its future. There is little point in moaning about the situation as it exists. We have to stir ourselves to change the situation, using every opportunity which presents itself. It is not enough to rest content with schemes designed to train journalists. The basis must also be created for their future work as tribunes of the people. We often editorialize about those who put the cart before the horse, forgetting that we often do the same. The organizations of editors and working journalists should formulate the perspectives we need, and implement schemes which will make it possible to reach them. The attempt at thinking aloud is only one of many. But when will we develop the energy and purpose to act? For unless we act, and very soon, in the interests of a truly independent and democratic Press, the giants-in-the-making will be impossible to control. Their "arrival" marks the total eclipse of the independent journalist, for even when the totalitarian State crushes them, it takes their place. We must act now. On this, there can be no two opinions.

10

Political Theories and Practices*

At whatever point in history we study them, political theories and practices reflect the dominant social conditions of the time and the play of various organized interests around the business of decision-making. The gulf between theory and practice is natural and invariably exists, sometimes large, sometimes less. Only when theory clashes frontally with practice, a confrontation ensues and sparks qualitative change. A collapse. A violent upset. A revolution.

Sometimes it is possible to measure the gulf between theory and practice. At other times, to assess the growing confrontation. Often, the process of confrontation and explosion builds silently, without the usual warning signals. The political process, thank goodness, cannot be computerized; it is too closely tied up with the emotions, heartbreaks and stirrings of men and women to be easily categorized or "programmed" as they say. This reality may change if society permits itself to be "systematized," but I seriously doubt this possibility despite the horrendous studies about the future.

I think these general remarks are necessary, I intend to avoid the usual course of presenting text-book knowledge about capitalist, socialist and mixed systems and then pointing out where the practice leads. I intend to mould the theme into a discussion

*From a talk delivered at the National Defence College, New Delhi, January 1976.

of our present predicament—and to show how the political theories and practices that are prevalent are way behind the challenges which have developed. The multi-pronged crises which affect every region of the world in various ways—developed, developing, underdeveloped, backward—is rooted in what I wish to term as the overall crisis of political theories and practices.

Let me range over the political bankruptcy in thought and action which we are witness to:

(a) In the so-called *capitalist world*, the myth built around special skills, full employment and unlimited growth has exploded. We know that the myth was based on an unjust past and on unequal trading. A hike in oil prices was enough to disturb the entire balance of the capitalist world. The mountains of petrodollars piling up in Arab accounts are on a scale that very soon the once affluent nations will have to fight liberation battles against the economic stranglehold of the Arabs! But, seriously, in the near future we will probably witness the total breakdown of capitalism as we have known it—that is, if wars are not waged in West Asia to re-establish the old order. Indeed, even if dependence on Arab oil is reduced through new and different technologies, or through the discovery of new oil bearing strata throughout the world, capitalist theory will undergo deep changes which will affect practice. It is too early to forecast the outlines of a non-socialist society, but we do know that the perspective of unlimited growth lies shattered, that many question marks have appeared over consumption patterns, and the maximization of profit is no longer the magic wand. At the same time, the multinational corporations are taking a look at themselves. They command immense resources and skills and may well detach themselves from the national interests of particular nations. Even in these limited areas of thinking, it is obvious that a greater degree of social control will have to be applied in the general interest, control which will affect the political theory of capitalism and its practice. A more socially oriented capitalism is on the agenda. At the same time, it needs massive democratic initiative to save these societies from fascistic envelopment.

(b) In the so-called *socialist world*, there has been a general failure to create perspectives of development qualitatively different from those of capitalism. The bourgeoisification of socialist societies is a marked features of our times—and now an obsessive campaign is under way in this region to match capitalist society in the supply of consumer goods, including private cars and the like. No diametrically different alternative has been spelt out. Only China, largely because of the population size, begins an experimentation with a simpler, austere way of living. It is an interesting start, but has yet to be tested politically, when Mao passes and a new generation of autocratic leaders rises. Socialist theory has thrown up a kind of state capitalism, and in the process it has not been able to guarantee dissent which is fundamental to a healthy dialectical method of thinking—thesis, anti-thesis, synthesis. Rigidity in theory and imitative practice are sought to be rationalized. Socialism no longer appears as a dramatically different alternative, only an interesting variation on a familiar theme. Indeed, even dynasties are developing in socialist lands. Witness Korea. In other words, profound revolutions have to spread to socialist movements in order to transform the egalitarian barrenness of socialist thought today. The European Marxists and even Communists are now raising critical issues which the Soviet Union cannot sidestep. In the course of this awakening, we may see a return of motivation and managerial skills to the socialist societies, a critical matter when one considers the surface of the earth now under "socialist control." Managerial failures here effect the entire world. Witness: Food imports by the USSR from USA. The future of revolutionary doctrine will depend on how ruling socialist or communist parties handle their political theory and practice.

(c) In the so-called *mixed systems*, it has become clear that so far they are essentially a screen, sophisticated or otherwise, to cover the manipulations of already entrenched and narrow vested interests. I say "screen," because the mixture of radicalism and status-quoism is such that no fundamental structural reorganization in a backward society is attempted. The mixed systems try to fuse the free enterprising of capitalism with the egalitarianism of socialism and end up by denying themselves the dynamics of both. This happens because adequate measures are not taken to insulate the experiment from powerful vested interests which operate through lobbies and through political parties. It would not be an exaggeration to say that the mixed systems, particularly those which zealously fight for democratic norms, demand a tremendous input of sustained thought, a constant testing of theory in the crucible of practice, and the ability to discard what does not work. This input is lacking in the developing areas where the mixed system is attempted. Even in India, more advanced than other developing areas, the mixed system was not backed with an adequate and sustained feed of ideas and concepts. It now provides a typical example of radical political posturing in support of what is tantamount to a dressed up *status quo*—or what is called Mercedes Benz Socialism. The correction of political theory and practice within a mixed system is perhaps more complex than in the capitalist and socialist systems—and the class alignments invariably tend to swing the system in the direction of Left or Right authoritarianism. The democratic infrastructure is too fragile and is easily subverted by ambitious cabals of leaders.

Surveying, broadly, the trends in the three differing areas of political theory and practice, it becomes quite clear that the world in general is facing a total breakdown of political institutions and that this breakdown is rooted in the economic anarchy that has been unleashed all over the world. I say "anarchy" because we have failed to take note of the incredible numbers of people seeking wasteful living standards even before the resources for humanity's basic needs have been made available. This race for more and more, so noticeable in the developed world, and visible among the ruling elites of the developing world, has created a situation which can only be described as crazy.

Democratization and egalitarianism have come to mean equal rights to wasteful standards—and on a highly individualistic basis. The cars packing the streets of western cities instead of public transport. The schools and universities growing with numbers, unable to give direction to education or to link with real needs. Medicine collapsing because we do not recognize how much of it can be self-administered. Housing barracks destroying environments because we fail to link town and village with rapid transport systems. And a huge demand for food and goods, actively sponsored by a cynical advertising industry, which destroys the very basis of a simple, satisfying and civilized way of life. Today, even a stabilization of population would not permit the wasteful standards we have given ourselves.

Just take stock of the facts of the global situation. Two-thirds of humanity is very much alive in squalor and misery, and growing in numbers, a reminder of the colossal task of development waiting to be tackled. To urge that this two-thirds live a simple life while the one-third goes on a luxury spree is to spark the kind of anger which could threaten the peace of the world. The theory that the world can live divided at two levels of living is as absurd as the view that there will always be rich and poor. These divisions are no longer tenable. New divisions around skill and responsibility will develop. The revolution in communications and expectations has brought global problems into a new focus. In other words, about the mundane question of living, we have to think in global terms about the resources that are available and the general standard of living that can be built on them for the peoples of the world.

The moment the debate is taken to this level of understanding, a totally different system of values comes into play.

We begin talking not of minimum standards for the not-so-fortunate, but of a single maximum standard for all—a point beyond which consumption is waste. This puts the onus on affluent areas to shed their luxuries, much in the manner of the rich being disciplined within a nation.

We begin talking not of individual housing and tidy plots, but of mass housing, of the link between rural and urban areas, of curbing urban growth, of anchoring rural populations by providing them a weightage of facilities and amenities, of using local construction materials, like mud, as against cement and steel, of the primacy of water and drainage for the mass of people.

We begin talking of transport not in terms of private cars, but buses. Mass transport. And rapid transit systems which permit working people to live in their original rural environment, moving into town daily. The slums, the shanty towns, the *jhuggies* and *jhompries* are bulldozed—not by brutal design but because they become irrelevant in the course of the transport revolution.

We begin talking of education very much in connection with the work to be done, both mundane and creative, and not in terms of meaningless degrees from meaningless universities. The search begins for education which increases communion between people, life-long education which is a natural part of living and renewal, and which does not create rival groups of Mandarins without any understanding of each other.

We begin talking of medicine and health at the grassroots. Ninety per cent of the diseases of man are curable by a simple pharmacopoeia, but ninety per cent of investment in medicine and health goes into tackling esoteric diseases or the ailments of elites trying to ward off death. Admittedly, health is a total operation, impinging on many activities, but the battle for health, mass health, is lost if there is no sustained effort to solve simple problems at the grassroots.

We begin talking of new national and international institutions and organizations which can cope with the problem of growing numbers. And this is no small problem. India, for example, will in twenty-five years, that is in the year 2000, be two Indias. A third India since independence. We cannot possible structure our life as it is today. If we do, we are asking for obliteration.

These are only some major elements of the new debate on political theories and practices, but it impacts willy nilly all ideologies and political beliefs. Those who close their eyes to the debate on the plea that it is "utopian" do damage to their own thinking, for it will remain linked to a *status quo* that is already collapsing. The future, I believe, is made up of a mix of utopias.

We are in the midst of a massive correction in thought and action throughout the world. Inflation, oil crises, trading in armaments, speculation in materials and resources, price manipulation and the like are merely symptoms of a general breakdown of the international system. The sooner we recognize this central fact the better. Delay in corrections will create only more complexity and more disorganization. Fortunately, during this transitional period, it is the more organized and advanced capitalist societies which will feel the pressure of the collapse. The socialist societies are able to cushion the economic shock in the initial stages, although politically the challenge to their rigid attitudes will mount, sparking unrest and instability. The still developing mixed system will probably not suffer unduly, particularly if they learn the lessons of the crisis and begin on the task of genuine democratic restructuring, not superficial planning by points.

And this brings me to India. I think it would be a good idea to apply some of these new theories to our complex reality and see how they would work out in practice. After all, as an advanced mixed system, we borrow theory and practice from both the capitalist and socialist. Now we are compelled to review our borrowing and to work for some degree of performance without which the very pressure of population will doom us to a series of disasters. What sort of conceptual framework, both in immediate terms and in perspective, should guide us? In the elaboration of such political theories and practices we shall be tackling questions which other nations too will face in their own way. And let me state here quite categorically that conceptually it is not possible to separate politics and economics.

1. There can be no beginning unless we face the breakdown of the political and administrative system. To put it mildly, it has shown incapacity, institutionally or in terms of accepted practice, to cope with the problems which are emerging. What we call harassment, delays, corruption and what have you is precisely this breakdown. It is the septic focus which politicians and citizens fattening on the *status quo* seek to hide. We have to find answers to this breakdown at every level, from the lavatory that does not work to the paralyzed minister. But declarations of emergency, the assumption of more and more power, the crushing of free opinion and dissent and talk about discipline and hard work as the answers to poverty make us look simplistic.

2. Politically, the parliamentary system just does not any more provide a valid expression for serious debate and

dissent. It has become a "business" based on the power of money. It has lost respect. It is no longer sacrosanct. A drastic reorganization has to be attempted to ensure respect for dissent which is the base of democratic functioning. And the beginning lies in a carefully thought out decentralization of decision-making and implementation.

3. Administratively, or institutionally, the States of India are too large, too populous, too sociologically complex. Built originally on the formula "One language One State," they have to be reorganized carefully. Some 50 to 60 States, manageable in size, expressing the felt needs of the coherent groups, would make for more sensitive governance. And that would mean the reassertion of the essential dignity of the citizen.

4. A restructured federal polity would require both a concentration of certain types of decision-making and a de-concentration of others. The perspective would inevitably have to be a wide delegation of power to break bottlenecks of various description. We are not Singapore, or Belgium or France or England. We are Europe. And it's time we understood the meaning of this.

5. Underpinning these qualitative political changes should be an equally qualitative re-definition of the society we intend building in this subcontinent, a society capable of feeding (with medicare!), housing (with transport!), and training (with employment!) a population of 1000 million by the year 2000 A.D., a society purged of its present elitist mentalities. Yes, a colossal economic task which correct political organization can assert.

I do not intend pushing myself into the field of answers. This is not an area for individual brain-waving, but solid collective endeavour to find a way out of the maze of problems around us. I am more interested in emphasizing that the sum of political theory and practice as we have known it in various parts of the world is inadequate, is failing us, and that we must stir to think afresh. The world is in the throes of the revolution of science and technology and it must command this revolution as once, not so long ago, the industrial revolution was commanded. We in India face both revolutions together, at the same time.

That's quite a challenge. In such a situation, we need to sensitivise ourselves to the future, to keep abreast with it—and not get caught in a tangle of slogans. Maybe we need to lay down certain minimum educational standards and expertise for our politicians, for they are the makers of confusion and chaos.

11

The *Bandh* Business*

The forward thrust of political energy in any society, particularly in those which are in the throes of fundamental development, is dependent on a host of factors and on how these are forged into a weapon of change by four political elements playing upon each other—the status-quoist, the catalyst, the agitator and the revolutionary polarizer. The strange, all-enveloping agitational form, the *bandh*, has to be understood in this context. It needs careful analysis if we are to determine its role in moulding political development. Such an analysis should also assist us in stripping the technique to its essentials and in determining what forces will influence this political agitation in India.

The subject of political agitation has, within the Indian setting, a very special significance. It involves a consideration of the fundamental concepts which hold this country together. These concepts are not the "obsessions" or "creations" of this or that leader, or this or that party. They evolved from the Indian reality, from the very nature of the freedom struggle and the kind of State we gave unto ourselves. Willy nilly, these concepts condition political-economic activity, agitational or status-quoist. First, the very sensitive federal character of our State which creates a continental consciousness. Second, the dominating role of the regional elites and specialized interests that an egalitarian sharing of economic resources be the basis for national develop-

*A talk delivered in 1970 at Delhi University.

ment. Third, the secular framework of policy and implementation.

These influences, which turn into concepts as we translate
them into the slogans of democracy, socialism and secularism,
can be neglected only at our peril. The unity of India is a frail
thing. It has been nurtured with much care during the Nehru
era and it is only logical that we grasp its very special elements
before we discuss specifically the nature of political agitation in
India.

It is for this reason that a conscious effort is continuously being
made at regional and central levels to create a national consensus
on policies. This Nehruist strategy—in many ways, similar to
the theorising on a single party system in other parts of Asia
and Africa—has fortified the original character of the Indian
National Congress, that is, an amorphous assembly of varied
opinions. Even opposition parties, including those with a so-called
Marxist-Leninist base, have, in one way or another, subscribed
to the politics of consensus. The differences between the parties
is normally on the degree of dynamism within the consensus.
A breakdown or erosion of the national consensus takes place
when a particular plateau of development is reached and preparations begin to ascend to the next plateau. For, vested interests
stand in the way of forward movement and have to be fought.

We are in such a phase now in economic terms. The job of the
ruling leadership is to forge a new consensus. The job of the
leadership of the opposition is to prevent the forging of such a
consensus on terms dictated by the entrenched interest of the
ruling party. This explains why the debate on political and
economic issues in India usually takes on the dimensions only
of a "family quarrel"; the confrontation is not total. Undoubtedly
this year agitations have been joined with a greater degree of
passion, even totality. There is a premium on them. Their fury
is engendered by sharp economic crises which coincide with the
political crises of an election year. But the effort continues to
reduce the tensions, to find points of contact between the warring
political factions. A total confrontation, however, is sought to
be avoided even by the extremists on Right and Left.

It is also necessary to view the problem of agitation from
the standpoint of the opposition parties. Several crucial considerations are at play:

First, the ruling party, although grown lazy and fat, continues to straddle the country and still manages to retain the cudos of being the party of Gandhi and Nehru, the party which won freedom. True, it has become infested with factions, the plaything of *dadas* of various description, the purveyor of patronage and privilege, but it manages to retain within its fold all manner of conflicting opinions, traditional and modern, capitalist and socialist, anarchic and cynical. This is its weakness and its strength—weakness when the opposition chisels its thinking and organization, strength when the opposition wallows in its own confusions.

Second, the business of building a parallel political machine to the ruling party is well-nigh impossible. Mass fronts are the weapon with which to erase the support of the party in power, but these mass fronts have the habit of developing regional characteristics. They have yet to assume a national image even at the level of *kisan sabhas* and *mazdoor sabhas*, despite the pretentious all-India labels which they flaunt. Movements which can easily cut across regions and embrace radicalized professionals—like a civil liberties movement—are seldom given the kind of general provocation to sustain them over a period of time. Activity against the ruling party is haphazard, splintered and very often parochial. Even the massive momentums of the linguistic agitations failed to nurture any solid continuing support for the opposition parties.

Third the challenge to the ruling party cannot be developed from one or two bases as is possible in other countries. India is criss-crossed by roads, and the network of towns permits the rapid concentration of police and military power at explosive points. Unless such power is widely scattered by a spreading agitation which takes roots in the country-side, no oppositional challenge has a chance of developing meaningful dimensions. This *bandh* business, confined largely to urban areas, carries its own limitations. Moreover, no 'long marches' are possible. The politico-geographical differences between India and China rule out mechanical equations. The story of the communist-led armed struggle in Telengana holds many lessons. No seizure of power is possible even in the classic Soviet revolutionary model, for what happens in Delhi need not condition developments elsewhere. Hence all agitations are short-lived, without the kind of political perspectives and emotional ballast which transform situations and institutions.

Fourth, the usual charges made against the mechanics of bourgeois democracy, which normally are so pertinent that they destroy faith in the relevance of the process, do not really make an impact on the Indian mind. Elections are free and without fear. The mass media, even where controlled by industrial empires, do not hold public opinion captive. The election process demands physical contact between candidate and voter. Communal and caste interests shape attitudes, particularly when no other issues emerge. Political education is rooted in the struggle to survive, not on complex economic and political formulations divorced from the Indian reality. Manipulation, where it exists, has not reached the point of destroying confidence in the democratic process. Impatience is confined to limited, isolated groups of radicals drawn from essentially middle class backgrounds. Unless something startling happens, this state of affairs will continue to prevail.

Fifth, the logic of the national consensus as the vital base of India's federal unity creates a massive "vested interest" in the present political system. It introduces into the Indian polity an element which the opposition parties are compelled to accept, but which they are unable to analyze within the known terms of ideological reference. Yet, a detailed analysis of the politics of consensus, and the techniques of agitation which arise from it, is necessary if the opposition parties pledged to the overthrow of the bourgeois State are to rediscover their manoeuvrability and flexibility. Every such attempt yields results which strike at the political dogmas of the Left. Because dogma is cherished, analysis is halted.

In other words, the content and present-day validity of the national consensus which has been built on the three pillars of secularism, democracy, socialism, the image which the ruling Congress Party has managed to preserve for itself in a country living in its villages, the obstacles to political growth faced by the opposition parties, and their own inhibitions about chalking out an Indian path of protest, change and transformation, create within the ranks of the agitators a deep frustration. This frustration fogs the mind, dulls it. It places a premium on opportunist postures, sometimes adventurist and sometimes conformist. It prevents full involvement in and commitment to a kind of sustained political battle which would lift the concept of Indian unity and progress to a new level. And, inevitably, it moulds the nature of political agitation in India, makes it hesitant, limited and parochial in the first stance—and then thoroughly romantic, adventurist and even anarchist in the next.

"Better chaos than the peace of the grave." Gandhi said something like that. But he said it when a foreign imperialism ruled. What is the relevance today?

It is possible to so arrange a series of simultaneous political explosions in a critical period—spreading from the towns to the villages —that the power of the Centre is dispersed and broken, and chaos sets in. But even this deliberate anarchist objective, which would splinter India's still frail unity, would require to be sustained and widespread before any tangible change could be effected politically. Haphazard *bandhs*, no matter how violent, cannot have any serious impact. They might change voting patterns, but only marginally, for the scale of disturbance in to-day's conditions is very much dependent on the degree of disarray within the ruling party and whether its rebel faction participates in the *bandh*. Moreover, this kind of disorganized, spasmodic activity tires the people, damages their essential interests, turns them against the agitators and, if unchecked, disarms them in the face of organized reaction.

Indeed, the pre-Independence struggles, which united the widest sections of the people, were more carefully and patiently organized by all parties. Always, meticulous arrangements were made to safeguard the interest of the people in the course of the struggle. The Telengana armed struggle of the Communist Party, soon after the transfer of power, embodied many of the lessons of the freedom struggle, the Tebhaga Movement in Bengal, the Patri Sarkar agitation of Maharashtra and Operation Paddy in Kerala. But it was the last of the organized struggles. Adventurism and short-cuts soon took over whether at the level of the general strike calls of the CPI in 1949 and 1951 or at the high points of the stir for the creation of separate linguistic states. A political or economic point was won or lost, but the ruling Congress Party weathered the storms. Even Kerala, where a Communist Government was voted to rule, witnessed the political incompetence of the most serious contenders for power.

Not without reason are comparisons drawn between the conscious, almost scientific, physical and spiritual preparations for the hunger-strike undertaken by Mahatma Gandhi and the comic demonstrations of today when apparently constipated gentlemen are surprised by their own incapacity to persist with the strike even before public attention has focussed on their ludicrous plight! Small wonder then that even claims of being on hunger-strike are disbelieved.

How, then, will this *bandh* business develop in the months ahead? It will, of course, lose its momentum once the general elections are held, but it would be politically inept to imagine that there are no dividends in *bandhs*. Any trade-union leader, who can command the closure of the transport services of a city, can be a skilled *bandhist* with the capacity to link his prestige to any significant political kite-flying. We are already witnessing *bandhs* of a sort employed in the factional warfare within the ruling party. But, whatever the future holds, it is clear that the opposition parties, whether of Right or Left, can only resolve their deep frustrations by taking up the organizational challenge of building a national confrontation to the ruling party. The health of Indian democracy is dependent on this.

There will be much theorization on how this confrontation can be built. It could be outside the ruling party, or within it, or both outside and within. By skilfully mounting pressure within the national consensus, it is possible to create a polarization which splits the ruling party, and its organization, across the country. Of course, it will be argued that the seasoned leadership of the ruling party is capable of adjusting to radicalization. This is all to the good. After all, polarization is not desired for its own sake. Alternatively, it is possible to create a new political formation which might within the context of this essentially middle class era cut cross political labels, analyze the reality that is India, and evolve the strategy and the tactics required to move this sprawling, complex, multi-communal State. But the nature of agitation and of confrontation will have to be conditioned by the politics of consensus for several decades to come—at least, until the cement of economic development has had time to settle and solidify, and the scientific-technological mind is in the ascendent. Until then there is no short-cut to power in an united, viable India.

Whatever shape future political development takes, and if the contestants for power in the subcontinent are disciplined by the paramount need to preserve the unity of federal India, there will be a constant searching for techniques of agitation which strike at status quoism but do not pull down what little democratic scaffolding we have set up over these twenty years. The *bandh* business has to be studied and analyzed in this context. Political sanctions demand organization—structure and institutions which provide the power to compel change. The persistent anarchic nature of political agitation in India today saps the strength of the people, makes them vulnerable to the appeal of charismatic adventurers, narrow-minded revivalists, those who imagine that all societies are doomed to function on the basis of masters and slaves whatever the phrases used to describe them. This is the critical challenge which has to be met.

12

Administration*

We have reached a critical phase in our continental development. Unfortunately, we have now also to cope with rather
strange transitory forms in our politics. Maybe, this is the
moment to focus on administration and administrators. Political
monoliths are dissolving, making possible perhaps the shaking
up of the administrative monolith. The transition we are witnessing will crystallize many challenges, but in all the alarums
and tensions we should not forget that the quality of administration is the key to accomplishing the goals we have set ourselves.

When discussing this subject of administration the impact of
the past, present and future must be a constant reference—and
invariably within the context of the Indian reality.

(a) *The past* needed a generalist who could exercise the
concentrated power of a largely feudal or colonial overlordship.

(b) *The present* demands a mix of generalists and specialists,
of perspective philosophers and hard-headed implementors,
together with a simplification of the cumbersome procedures
which have been built up under democratic accountability or
what is called the delegation of power and decision-making.

(c) *The future* will call for dedicated, involved men who
combine in themselves both generalist-specialist qualities and

*A talk to officers of the ICS and IAS, New Delhi, 1971.

who function boldly and autonomously under a massive decentralization of power.

I am going to concern myself largely with the present, drawing
on the past and dipping into the future. I shall not go over
familiar ground, detailing what is wrong with the system. It is
my belief that our administrative system has managed to gather
unto itself the worst qualities of various systems, particularly the
colonial which treated everyone as incompetent, inferior and dishonest—except those, of course, who reached the top. This
system of ours, in my opinion, is the major obstacle to national
progress.

Let me, then, sketch some essential steps which are required
to extricate us from the predicament in which we find ourselves.
I shall detail the major reforms in some order of priority:

(*a*) A rigorous exercise must be carried out to demarcate
clearly three types of jobs which the administrator will have
to cope with—regulatory/coordinatory; promotional/growth-
oriented; and commercial/profit-based. Each type requires its
own special skills. The administrator must choose his skill or
be placed in one or the other category on the basis of past
performance. Such an exercise may well spark the need for
three specialized services of administrators. Vested interests—
individual or group—cannot be allowed to hold up this
reform. The attempt at the moment to saddle administrators
with this or that kind of job creates an uncertain creature who
almost invariably blocks growth, hampers performance. It is
not so much his fault that he is what he is, but of the system
which has not been reformed for the tasks of today.

(*b*) Jobs imply tasks. The tasks I have detailed need three
types of institutions. The regulatory/coordinatory function
must of necessity be performed by the government department. The promotional/growth oriented function is best conducted by autonomous bodies subsidized by the concerned
ministries and accountable to Parliament for the utilization
of the grants they receive. The commercial/profit-based activity should be entrusted fully to totally autonomous corporations drawing their funds from the banking institutions of the
state and under ministerial scrutiny only for performance. In

other words, three distinct institutional forms must be utilized
to carry out three distinct administrative tasks. You cannot
mix the functions or move men from one to the other network.

(*c*) Procedures and the design of work for each of these
institutionalized set-ups will vary. Indeed, there will be nothing in common between the framework within which the
regulatory/coordinatory function is performed and that in
which the commercial/profit-based activity takes place.
"Nothing" means nothing. I know that all manner of stereo-
typed arguments about "accountability" can be advanced, but
I would like to remind those who think of advancing them to
remember that all the procedures in the world can be circum-
vented—and are, all the time! So let's stop imagining that
there is magic in bureaucratic *mantras*. The only magic we
should search for is performance—and it doesn't lie in the
lowest tender! The showing in India is poor, very poor—despite the press releases of public corporations and the un-
necessarily large advertisements! We must change this state of
affairs, not by circumventing rules but by changing the rules.
Only then can we work without the paralyzing fear of CBI
interventions, fair and foul. . .

(*d*) Employment in public enterprise, in a country like
India where jobs are scarce, cannot be turned into a sinecure.
Performance norms must be maintained or sacking must take
place. Public enterprise today is just becoming the refuge of
those who imagine that they have a job for life irrespective of
performance. This notion needs shattering if we wish to survive as an enlightened society. In other words, rights must be
matched by responsibilities. We are very far from this goal
and muddle-headed, pseudo-socialist thinking is only helping
to create more confusion by talking only of "rights."

(*e*) Following upon these measures, if we are to learn from
the past, it is imperative that financial powers be delegated to
Union Ministries and through them to the three types of institutions coordinated or guided by them. The delegation should
be observed in the budgeting for the year. Any excess over the
allotted budget should be coordinated and adjusted by the
Union Cabinet. The delegation of financial powers is the key
to successful performance. We should not take any talk of

administrative reform seriously until this delegation is carried out. The matter has been engaging the attention of the government for some time, but, as always, a final decision keeps getting postponed.

(*f*) In this connection, Parliament also needs to revise attitudes to public enterprise. The strange passion of politicians and MPs to dip their fingers into the day-to-day running of enterprises is unhealthy and does vast damage to the delicate fabric of management. Even the parliamentary committees (PAC and PUC) are functioning in a manner which is wasteful and ineffective. Scrutiny is necessary, but of essentials, and no cheap publicity points should be registered until the facts have been checked. The flabbiness of government has permitted a process of questioning which is most questionable. Parliament should review its role vis-a-vis public enterprise—and, for general interest, the present cost of the PAC and the PUC should be separately shown in the accounts of public undertakings!

I have spoken of the major reforms which suggest themselves in the course of studying administrative practice, past and present. Now, let us move to the vital minor reforms without which the major reforms would be nullified.

(*a*) Recruitment must become an exercise in justice and fair play. This seems like the great cliche of our age! Invariably I find that when the observance of procedures is probed, the "fixing" usually begins with the way the advertisement for a job is drafted. The opportunities for "fixing" don't end there. Candidates have to be selected, interviewed, put on probation etc. Sometimes the procedures are observed only to declare that no one suitable applied. Then, there is freedom to "fix." These generalizations are backed by much research done at various levels. The spirit of public service has been vitiated by this kind of operation.

(*b*) Once the most talented have been recruited, how do we ensure that they are not reduced to ciphers. In the absence of "democracy," it was possible to work out some kind of system to ensure a modicum of fair play. Now, illiterate, power-hungry ministers put pressure on senior officers who are careerists—

and in this way break the back of upright freshers. In other institutions, even those which are autonomous, senior executives flout the rules to surround themselves with yes-men and the like. Talent and independence are not rewarded. Only that object called "loyalty" in the vocabulary of the bureaucracy is rewarded. Patterns are, therefore, set which are difficult to change. We must, in other words, set up internal procedures to reward talent and performance—and ensure that the non-conformist will not be punished.

(*c*) I do not claim to know the answers, but it is clear that a marked deterioration in standards is visible. In the days when the imperialist British ruled, I believe one out of 28 was promoted. The figure was more like one out of 8 a few years ago under the monolithic Congress raj. Today, it is one out of 3 or 4! This is an absurd situation for a society which has to place the emphasis increasingly on competence and efficiency. It is also revealing. The structuring of performance reports and confidential reports is out-dated. In the old days, when the quantum of staff was infinitesimal compared to the situation prevailing today, this reporting was adequate. No longer. Now, questionnaires must be scientifically expanded to prevent lazy, prejudicial or incorrect reporting. There must be built-in checks within the questionnaires to prevent distortions and abuse. In this context, personnel departments need considerable strengthening. And what is more, we need to mechanize our systems. If the government is pushed to use computers to locate talent, there seems to be a good case to look into the possible programming now! Appointments at high and low levels continue to be made on mere hunches and personal likes and dislikes. A widespread feeling of insecurity results in the absence of just, fair and understanding leadership. This is a major danger to public enterprise in our country.

(*d*) Insecurity gives birth to two evils. The *first* is the tendency deliberately to favour docile second-raters to more angular and difficult first-raters. Dynamic and competent deputies are not favoured, for fear that they may take over! Wherever you go in government enterprises, the gulf between the Number One and the Number Two is too wide. It is unhealthy and we must fight this tendency within ourselves and in others. The second tendency develops unconsciously because of the continental nature of recruitment in India. I refer to the lack of psychological *rapport* or understanding which blocks the growth of solid relationships between executives and prevents the building of a coherent leadership. This is due mainly to the fact that personnel are drawn from widely differing cultural backgrounds and almost unconsciously colleagues develop antipathies towards each other which they then try to explain away in terms of incapacity of adjustment between an orthodox Tamilian and a pushing Punjabi! This kind of problem is going to remain with us for a long time. Possibly, it will grow worse in the period now unfolding because of sharp regional biases. All the more reason to be on guard and to find remedies in public enterprises.

(*e*) Deputationists are a threat to the health of autonomous corporations. They are fundamentally "outsiders" who block the internal growth of the corporation. As birds of passage they introduce a cynical, careerist attitude. I could understand the need for deputationists if they possessed some extraordinary skills. Their main ability appears to be a capacity to avoid transfer from one location to another and to steer through a jungle of rules and regulations. This "steering" is a costly business and we want an end to the jungle—and, therefore there is little point in calling for the skill of the deputationist. These remarks apply equally to financial advisers and accounts experts. I will say nothing about the way in which the deputationist system has been used to entrench vested interests, to make personal issues dominant in national undertakings, and to build up perks for a favoured few.

(*f*) Constant training and retraining, solidly India-based, must also become a feature of the administrative services. In the past, a balance of challenges was presented to the administrative officer in the course of his career. Today, willy nilly, a certain kind of specialization takes place—but at a very superficial plane. The injection of training courses helps to sift cadres for more scientific placing, keeps personnel open and receptive to the new and the fresh. This is vital in a rapidly changing world where the revolutions of science and technology are transforming our concepts and ideas. India, I am afraid, has not begun to face these problems. We think we

have. We are terribly self-satisfied. But the world comes visiting and smiles at our illusions. The demand for modernization must be built from below. It must be articulated by the
juniors who will inherit the forbidding world of tomorrow.

(g) Union activity in public enterprises is a racket. All
manner of illiterate "outsiders" have moved in to use union
control to feather their nests. Many a public enterprise is
held to ransom by these "trade unionists." The government,
as owner of a vast and sprawling industrial and commercial
empire, must establish norms specifically for public enterprise.
The private and public sectors cannot be equated. Most
energetic steps must be taken to correct the terrible distortions which have taken place in unions concerned with the
public sector. Government flabbiness and opportunist interference by MPs and MLAs have created an explosive situation.
Until this mess is cleared, we cannot even begin to think of
worker participation in management on any considerable
scale. It would become a racket in the hands of dishonest
outsiders determined to block public enterprise.

The modernization of administration demands not only the utilization of all the new mechanical aids to effectiveness and efficiency, but research in depth by men who are innovators, not
imitators. This is easier said than done. Such research calls for
close cooperation between various disciplines concerned with
behaviour patterns. No work of this kind is being done in our
country. Indeed, so much of the theorizing done on Indian
administration is superficially correct but needs to be linked more
integrally with Indian realities. To take one example, it is worth
investigating why the Indian is so hostile to the idea of "coordination!" May be, he would perform better when not coordinated and interfered with. A vast enlightenment would take place
if we could unravel such a mystery. Take another: competitive
public enterprises. Two HSLs; Two IACs. May be three! India,
after all, is a continent. I hope that increasingly this research
will be conducted by men who are not mere theorists like me but
who have some practical experience—and this should not be
considered as a plea for the bureaucratic control research!

13

Poverty of Nations or Notions*

Economists, sociologists and political scientists have, for some-time now, been groping for an understanding of the multitude of trends and counter-trends which make up post colonial Asia. Much of the writing is highly speculative and reveals huge gaps in the knowledge of the experts who manage to gather the funds and facilities to undertake their researches. Naturally, when Myrdal began his study, wide-spread interest developed. He had a reputation. A large number of specialists from several countries assisted him. A twenty year experience was to be cove-red. We now have three considerable volumes impressively titled *Asian Drama, an Inquiry into the Poverty of Nations*, a massive theme backed by a ten year effort at analysis.

In the Foreword, we are promised an argument which "goes against the grain of much contemporary thought, cuts deep, and moves at a level where differences of opinion are fundamental." "For Professor Myrdal had not only to move against accepted premises and assumptions; what was more difficult, he had to move against those premises which he had himself done so much to establish and to make seem self-evident."

In the Prologue, Myrdal himself takes over to assault the frame within which all Asian studies have sought to be stuffed, a deadly, self-defeating process which has so often made a mockery of research in this region. The frame has been so

*From *Yojana*, May 1968.

buttressed by the intellectual elite of the west that anyone dar-
ing to break it has invited ridicule. Making a powerful plea for
"the sociology of knowledge, which is concerned with causa-
tion," Myrdal sketches the history of "The Beam in Our Eyes"
and promises to uncover the reality. Undoubtedly, a tremendous undertaking when dealing with the congealed view of a
sprawling continent about which the inhabitants themselves are
somewhat confused.

Asian Drama, an Inquiry into the Poverty of Nations, in three
volumes, is to be the catalyst for future research, a major break-
through or take-off, comparable by implication and suggestion
to the pioneering works of former unravellers of truth. The
"present book is intended to be undiplomatic," says Myrdal.

In our study we want to step outside the drama while we are
working. We recognize no legitimate demand on the student
to spare anybody's feelings. Facts should be stated coldly.
Understatements, as well as overstatements, represent biases.
In this book we argue that there is a need not merely for
qualifications and reservations, but for a fundamental change
in approach.

The "drama" is explained. The reader cannot help but res-
pond to the excitement promised. The curtain rises. The Introduction. Something is wrong. Maybe, the uneasy apprehension
usual to first acts. No. Something is wrong. The promise is
forgotten. The jungle that is Asia is entered. The track is lost.
A confident movement in this direction and that, but soon to be
engulfed by the jungle. The unraveller of truth either does not
possess the weapons to take on the jungle or is fearful of what
might lie beyond. The old cliches are trotted out and shot down,
not for the first time. The new cliches are dressed up. The footnotes begin to tell their dreary story. This is another card-index
job. And those who have read the literature of the post-colonial
era find themselves re-reading the material in a kind of sum-
marized mix. Even that old mutton, "Asian Values," is served
up and India seen as the chief chef. . .

It is with a certain sadness that one begins to plough through
unending pages of the mix. It would not be fair to take each
section of out-dated thought and highlight the new research

already published which finds no mention even in the footnotes. Myrdal, and his younger collaborators, must believe that Asia and thinking on Asia is much the same as it was ten years ago when they moved around in the region. There has been an explosion of knowledge since then and they are unaware of it. If Marx suffered, in the words of this book, from a "systematic bias," Myrdal appears lost in the economic-political-social jungle that is Asia, finding himself a victim of mechanical computerization.

In Myrdal's thesis, it was only to be expected that India would take a major position. The material for computerization is plentiful and easily available. The rest of Asia is reduced to peripheralism. As for China, it doesn't really make an impact! The supposedly subtle generalizations on the Indian subcontinent which provide the "new" analysis with a "new" frame are extraordinary to say the least. "In India, and in Pakistan as well, it is now generally recognized that not only the unification of British India but also the measure of political integration that made possible the creation of two independent states, was the result of the last hundred years and more of British rule. . ." The idea of partition "took root and flourished mainly because of the religious split between Muslims and Hindus and the communal conflicts stirred up by extremists in both groups. . ."

Speaking of the India-China border, "India has chosen to appeal to International Law to justify frontiers fixed by an imperial policy the Indian Congress movement denounced in its younger day. . ."

By contrast, India's determination to remove the French and Portuguese from their precarious footholds on the subcontinent implied a demand for slightly more than its territorial inheritance from Britain. In fact, India and other Asian states have tended to apply a double standard of judgement to territorial questions. They regard colonial possessions within their borders as permanent aggressions, which they are prepared to deal with forcibly when it is to their advantage and within their power to do so. But they are quite legalistic when it comes to justifying their own inherited frontiers against neighbouring states, even though these boundaries took little or no account of ethnic, cultural or linguistic criteria. . .

The war in the Himalayas in 1962 sparks comments like, "The Indian public was offered a variety of reassuring reasons for the sudden Chinese withdrawal" and "Some Indian commentators managed to interpret the Chinese withdrawal as a Chinese defeat. . ." "The decision to secure foreign military aid raised doubts abroad and at home about the traditional Indian policy of non-alignment in world affairs, but the collapse of the China policy has dissipated the moral and emotional climate surrounding this concept. . . Only rarely does anyone in India other than the disreputed and now mostly imprisoned leaders of the pro-Chinese wing of the Communist Party express the view that Indian policy in its conflict with the Chinese may not have been a hundred per cent right."

I could go on like this, but it is a tedious exercise. Either Myrdal has not understood the ramified situations or, in his desire to be fresh, has fallen into the trap of recording opinion which others have refrained from only because it does not stand the test of facts. Perhaps, political understanding of Asian trends is too bewildering. A more rigorous economic approach within the context of an inquiry into the poverty of nations might have revealed the path through the jungle. But even this, I am afraid, would not have salvaged the Myrdal thesis. For, as one begins to push through the economics section, the same computer approach with a limited reference, is apparent. Indeed, the poverty of nations is inquired into without any solid reference to the depradation of the colonial era—a fashionable tactic in these days when our world is being increasingly polarized between the rich and poor nations, and when poverty is sought to be presented out of historical context, a reflection of basic incapacities.

India, according to Myrdal, is what he calls a "Soft State." There is dichotomy between ideas and reality. "The tendency is to use the carrot, not the stick." The level of social discipline is low. All this is rationalized and extolled, a la Gandhi. Ideals are important, but must await a change of heart. Conservative and reactionary forces are strengthening. "The persistence of the caste structure in Indian society provides a striking example of the divergence of precept and practice." But, can half truths make up a thesis?

Significantly, Myrdal's search has not taken him to the core of the problem—the complexity of the Indian polity, the specific features of an evolving federal democracy, the fact that in many ways the experiment is a pioneering one. We have learned during the tortuous post-war years that there are no magic wands to wish away poverty. Growth carries within itself the seeds of new and even more explosive tensions in our sprawling societies. Certain priorities have to be located. Gaps in development have to be bridged. Defences have to be erected against the marauding activities of the more powerful nations. The scientific and technological revolution has to be understood in terms of Asian realities. Myrdal opens no doors. He is merely the recorder of failures already recorded. The truth remains unrevealed, despite the promise of the Foreword, the Prologue and the Introduction. And nothing illustrates this better than the economic section of these three volumes.

In this, Myrdal attempts to set out the basic features of economic geography in South Asia. Agriculture continues to be "the dominant branch of production." The population density is roughly the same as that of Europe, excluding the USSR, and about four times that of the USA. The man/land ratio is not strikingly high—half that of China, and much lower than in Japan. Low productivity in agriculture is the key to low economic development. Population density is closely related to the cropping pattern and the pattern of agriculture. Population growth causes fragmentation of holdings and increases the relative number of landless and the poor. Plantations were, in fact, a process of industrialization, that this aspect is neglected in most discussions diminishes the emphasis on agriculture. European ownership prevented a diffusion of skills. Middlemen or "oriental aliens" were used. Manufacturing industries did not develop. Crafts declined or were destroyed by the colonial masters of Asia. Dealing with these "economic realities," Myrdal comes to the conclusion that "rigid social stratification" and the absence of rationalism, institutional and attitudinal, accounted for the stagnation in South Asia! Nothing more, nothing less.

The thesis continues. Myrdal distinguishes three kinds of splits in South Asian societies—level and character of civilization between dominant ethnic groups and tribal peoples; the contest between modern, market-oriented and profit-seeking forms of economic enterprise and the traditional subsistence

economy; the ethnic cleavage resulting from migratory movements, particularly of the Chinese and Indians. He considers
them extreme examples of "plural" societies: the various groups
mix but do not combine. Hence, minority problems! As you can
see from this summary of a section, the approach is mechanical
and the conclusions arrived at are essentially rooted in a frame
which it is not possible to place on Asia, neither the whole nor
a portion of it. Much of the research and analysis, which our
part of the world has been subjected to, has been vitiated by a
refusal on the part of the foreign expert to accept the possibility of the frame itself being irrelevant.

The "Soft States" and the "plural societies" of Asia are now
to be gathered together as a regional model. These border on
the preposterous, for Asia is likely to yield a series of models.
European experience is relevant only to the extent to which it
throws light on this or that aspect of growth—for example, the
rise of regional languages and their enthronement in India. The
problem of Asia as a continent is locked in the scientific and
technological revolution. Is it possible for the continent to make
up the leeway of centuries by imitating processes in developed
regions? Does the built-in leap effect of this scientific and technological revolution, deny land masses like India and China the
possibility to compete in growth? Are we doomed to a growing
polarization? What are its consequences?

These fundamental questions do not occur in this analysis
even as the backward Asians are grappling to search for answers, admittedly at a theoretical level. Nehru was obsessed by
this searching. Mao's obsession saw expression in the cultural
revolution. Vital questions have been posed and they are integral to an inquiry into the poverty of nations but foreign ex-
pertize seems to fall into a frame of investigation which has,
time and again, proved its total inadequacy.

Where Myrdal is on firmer ground is the poverty of statistics.
But of what use are accurate statistics, if the conceptual
approach to national output and the structure of the economy
is misleading? On this basis, "Burma has exhibited by far the
fastest rate of growth." At the end of the 1950s Burma was
classed as an economy well on the way to success. Pakistan,
Thailand and Ceylon are stagnant in terms of output per head.
The Phillippines is showing fairly rapid growth. As for India,

its income per head is supposed to have fallen, although there was marginal improvement during the latter half of the fifties.

The mystery in Asian statistics makes Myrdal somewhat hesitant as he presents his tables. Inevitably, the subliminal conclusion comes through. The countries with plantation economies have a future. This puts a big question mark over India and Pakistan. But surely, Myrdal realizes that the rationalization of agricultural techniques even in a non-plantation agriculture, as in the Punjab, can work miracles. Today, we know what miracles have been worked. Admittedly, the agricultural revolution under way in India, too recent to have found a place in the thesis, may lead to a new-type plantation economy, but there is nothing to suggest that this is inevitable.

As for the industrial sector, it was customary to speak of it in terms of cottage, small-scale and large-scale. Myrdal continues to see the future in these terms, although he puts them into new envelopes marked "mainly traditional," "mixed" and "mainly modern" and divides the product between them. There is no realization of the possibility that these three sectors of the growing industrial complex of South Asia can be fused in any sensitive planning for the revival of a continent.

A great deal of perceptive thinking has begun on linking the craftsmen to the national market, a step which builds integral living standards and prevents the directionless movement of masses of people to the towns. Small scale industry, rural based, solves a series of problems related to rapid growth. Indeed, the thesis of accelerating the growth of factories, even in the future, must be fought if we are to salvage the quality of life. Asia may fail, and pass through the same traumas which afflict the advanced regions, but Myrdal might have tackled this aspect of Asian thinking with a greater sensitivity and depth.

The argument on levels of living, saving and inequality, foreign trade and capital flows, the whole subject of varied conditions in the region is a familiar one. The obvious is stated, a mass of research already done is collated but the conclusions drawn are astonishingly ordinary. Twenty years of attempted independent activity have convinced even the elites of Asia that the normal approach to the problems of poverty and development hold no salvation for the mass of Asian peoples living in homes which are little more than shelters from the elements.

When Myrdal talks about the need to pursue "resolute development policies" and says that "it is probable, however, that on the Indian subcontinent social inequality is more pervasive and more detrimental to free competition, in the wider sense of the term than anywhere in the western world in recent centuries," he is revealing the bias which colours his whole thinking on the subject. The bias becomes a developing dogma when he states: "We are thus led to the major question of whether in South Asia today, the complex of political, social and economic institutions and the attitudes underlying and deriving from those institutions represent greater inhibitions and obstacles to development than did those in the western world in earlier times." Even though he admits that no parallel investigations have been conducted into the past of western countries—as if parallelism is possible in terms of colonial plunder!—he believes that attitudes and institutions are less favourable.

Had Myrdal been bolder in his probe, he would have detailed the role of colonialism in building the vital surplus for the industrialization of the west, he would have understood that aid to Asia is seen by Asians as a debt repaid, he would have noted in depth the hidden exploitation inherent in present day aiding operations, he would have compared these aiding operations with the Soviet assistance to Communist China which has received, despite the propaganda, a balanced industrial base. He would then have realized what is wrong with the unbalanced development of countries like India despite all the efforts of the planners, and he would perhaps have indicated pointers to remedial action. The newness of his approach, so widely advertised in the world's press, appears to merge into a neglect of history, past and present.

The over-worked tale of India's failures might have been disciplined with the inclusion of a solid analysis of India's successes, despite the sudden and crippling burden of defence imposed from 1962—a burden which even today, in proportionate terms, terrified Japan. There is no comprehension of the fact that, once the secret of motivating millions of people is discovered, results can be quick. Hence, one finds no reference to the possibility of India's agricultural breakthrough, now generally admitted, or of the fact that over large areas the merits of various birth control measures are discussed as once the merits of local medicine used to be. On the contrary, Myrdal says: "A spontaneous spread of birth control practices is not in prospect." That presumably also applies to new agricultural techniques; a theory which our farmers are at the moment busy blowing up.

Management remains a problem but not as Myrdal sees it—not a matter of cadres but of organization. It is best to confine ourselves to the Indian example, for the volumes under review concentrate largely on the Indian drama. A vast subcontinent has to be developed. There are pulls and pressures from each region within a political system which, despite Myrdal's question-marks, is democratic in terms of sanctions through a free franchise. The last general election is a pointer. If there are no institutions at the base of the pyramid of power, it is clear that the system cannot ignore the base. Since 1962, a point in time at which Myrdal seems to have disconnected with the region apart from turning the pages of a few journals, a basic reassessment of goals, priorities and policies has been under way. If no coherent planning has emerged, it is because the complexities are weighing heavily on the solution seekers. There is not an idea in Myrdal's survey of planning, labour utilization and the population explosion which has not been under debate and scrutiny. This is a salutary fact particularly when it is made out that Asia or India, in fact, is suffering from "verbal fuzziness."

Programmatic planning is now being influenced by pragmatic considerations; indeed, the danger is that there may be too great a swing towards unprincipled pragmatism in the interest of the dominant sections. If planning from below has not developed, it is because a whole group of economists drawn from various persuasions and associated with India's Planning Commission seldom moved beyond the mechanical application of western experience. They were unable to link creatively the traditional rural based industry of our land to the national market or were reluctant to espouse concepts which would be considered primitive.

Myrdal swings towards Gandhian attitudes and then attempts to link these with capitalist farming. We cannot be so naive. The realities of political behaviour in a subcontinent warn us that even as the new agricultural strategy makes its impact there is danger of a sharp polarization at the rural base. The Gandhians, or those of them who are still close to the village, are already working to find the answers to this growing polarization, for they realize the threat it holds to the unity of a developing subcontinent. This does not appear as an issue in Myrdal's thesis, except in the diffused form of what is called "political stability."

If the unity of the subcontinent emerged as an issue, and if Myrdal had more thoroughly understood the explosive content of growth in terms other than "employment and unemployment," "backwash effects," "dependancy burdens," "climatic considerations," "traditional corruption," "traditional idleness" and "qualitative demography," he might have linked himself more closely to the actual reality and been less cavalier in dismissing the gains of these twenty years. The concentration on industrialization, and the implied interdependence of one region on another, has provided the base for the parallel emergence of a technological and scientific agriculture and created a viable stake in continental unity, a stake which willy nilly disciplines the outwardly mercurial political transition which federal India is making. Even a federal Europe, with all its sophistication and affluence, would not be able to support a central government embracing state governments which owe allegiance to all manner of ideologies. Foreign experts need to ponder on these rather obvious facts before they jump to conclusions like, "it is difficult to be optimistic about the future" or that India is democratic "in a fashion" or that "no improvements in standards are possible." And this is not an attempt to minimize the failures and criticisms of which there are many.

The attempt to place the entire blame for economic failure on Asian society and leadership arises from a refusal to analyze the role of foreign capital, foreign aid, foreign interference and foreign ideas. These are vital elements in the policy-mix of an open and vulnerable society such as Inda. It appears as if Asia is living in a kind of self imposed vacuum and is free to operate the "rational" policies suggested by Myrdal. The interpretation of social practices is outdated and statistics are made to serve the thesis as when drought is not mentioned in connection with the fall in agricultural production in India during 1965-66. The extraordinary suggestion that the use of fertilizer in irrigated areas might damage output in the dry areas by diverting this input implies a non-belief that it is possible to produce special seed precisely for these areas—a fact which our agricultural scientists will record perhaps, before this year has been rung out. Similar is the cynicism which surrounds the commentary on the rural works programme. A massive creative potential is available, but it is not so simple to create a continental motivation.

Myrdal is more lucid when he attacks the refusal to transform property relations and the social structure. Admittedly, in comparative terms, the rich have grown richer and the poor poorer, but the people of India know how much their lot has improved over twenty years, despite the maze of statistics. A more rigorous thrust in this direction is on the agenda now that India is making the political transition to a genuine federal policy. If this transformation is not unleashed by political pressure or for the reason that Myrdal advances—that the opportune revolutionary moment has passed—then may be a capitalist, Japanese-style path of development is opening but, again, this thought is not sparked by the researches embodied in these volumes.

Repeatedly, Myrdal stresses the "unsuitability of western concepts" when analyzing South Asia, but he falls into a western framework without realizing it. This is part and parcel of the intellectual standstill which we are witnessing the world over—the utter failure to evolve a more meaningful frame of reference for development and growth. The obsession with the population explosion is only a reflection of this. Even as we tackle this explosion, we have to think beyond it. If change is sought, then that change must change man. Only then can two-thirds of mankind—the depressed and the deprived—recover hope. The western model of affluence can no longer inspire. The phenomenon of the "flower children" made this clear to those who think in Asia. Even in the aberrations of the Maoists, there is a kernel of truth.

And so we move on to the investment in man, in his health and his education. Myrdal covers a vital area which, in a sense, he helped to highlight in his earlier work, but his vision is limited. True, health and education cannot be separated, for the brain has to absorb knowledge and skills and the body must have the energy to implement the tasks of productivity. But, for

Asia, there is more in health and education. This emerging continent has to nurture societies which are capable of projecting a value system which avoids the waste and decadence of developed nations. This is not just a moral judgement, but an essential economic consideration if two-thirds of mankind is to emerge from its depressed condition. Is bourgeoisification inevitable? Can the poor nations of Asia be persuaded to skip a whole experience? Is it possible to prepare prototypes of good living which are more civilized and conserve the limited resources of the underdeveloped world? Would these new prototypes be able to defeat the accepted models of living in a shrinking world?

These questions are pertinent because they directly impact the foundation of policies. To ignore them at this stage in development is to invite despair, for Western affluence cannot be recreated in nations embracing 500-800 million peoples—at least, not in the lifetime of these peoples. The foreign expert needs to look at the world from Delhi and Peking rather than from London, Washington and Stockholm. Then, perhaps, he would begin to understand the trauma that thinking Asians, Africans, and Latin Americans are experiencing. Too long have we listened to views which have no perspective relevance to our condition. Without commitment to perspectives which make simple sense, the will to break-through is blunted. This is the common experience of the underdeveloped world. Even Myrdal's sympathetic study of Gandhi did not create a new dimension in his thinking.

I have deliberately avoided plunging into detailed rebuttals of so many generalizations, for then this review would have taken the shape of another book. Detailed debates on various aspects of Myrdal's approach will no doubt become commonplace as soon as these three volumes are generally available. But it is clear that "the inquiry into poverty of nations" has yet to be written. May be it will be necessary to produce three volumes on "the poverty of notions" as a preliminary preparation.

14

Wanted : An Integrated Society*

Minimum control and maximum freedom! Undoubtedly, this is an ideal for which the most sensitive humans have searched since the beginnings of collective developmental effort. Wherever one turns, the same striving is visible, even among those who are at the moment most controlled—the Communist societies which repeatedly proclaim their faith in the ultimate withering away of the state apparatus. How to ensure that the dream does not dissolve, that we do not become our own crucifiers, that is the question. Unfortunately, we have as yet not even attempted to face it.

In the economically developed or affluent west, the rise of giant industrial cartels, of sprawling and congested cities, of complex and ramified organizational forms, has reduced man, the maker of it all, to the level of the marvellous machines he creates. Leisure—genuine, creative leisure—continues to evade the people of the west; increasingly, they find themselves in the hands of psychiatrists who have become the "general practitioners" of affluent society. And not without reason, for life has become a horrible kind of nightmare, a vicious business which revolves around the problem of "getting on."

Amateur and professional sociologists write books on the subject of modern twentieth century man. He is an extraordinarily dull creature. He fills his home with every conceivable

*From the *Swarajya* Special Issue, January 1962.

gadget, one more intricate than the other. He goes in for more and bigger cars, chromium-encrusted to suit his new tastes. His fashions in dress, food, drink and relaxation are dictated by the profit motive of the consumer goods industry, and he accepts the dictation because he himself has come to believe that such things constitute "the good life." He is part and parcel of the waste-making mania of the west. If he should hesitate to join the "spree," there are banks and hire-purchase societies to break down his initial resistance.

For the most part, the sociologists who analyze these phenomena claim that the only solution is to make man aware of his folly, to educate him. But, significantly, very few attempt to explain that "the good life," as we understand it today, is the opiate which creates the nightmare of "getting on." In fact, the media of mass communication in the West are largely organized to prevent such a realization from gaining acceptance. The argument has a familiar ring: if you do not have the incentive of "getting on," then the tempo of economic progress slackens and "the good life" recedes.

This dynamic, senseless, awe-inspiring, futile effort to produce more and to consume more, to compete with everyone on the street, to take that competition into the home itself, creates the tensions referred to earlier and also the oppressive and corrupt machines of organization and enforcement of laws and regulations and responsibilities which is driving modern man to despair. Is this the only perspective—the rat race?

Some of us turn our attention to the socialist world. We condone the brutalities of the class war hoping that they will help to end the exploitation of man by man, create more equal opportunities, more equality. We condone the vast bureaucratic machine, believing that once the era of plenty dawns, this machine will wither away with the state. We condone the personal faction fights, the national rivalries, implying that these are carry-overs, from a selfish past, that they too will be transformed. We condone all this vaguely, confident that socialist society will give birth to the new man, the integrated human, the scientist-philosopher, the man with a mind and a heart. But... what is the reality?

Despite attempts to remove the main barriers to dissent in the more prosperous regions of the socialist world, despite the growing attack on the administrative and oppressive powers of the giant bureaucracy of both State and ruling party, despite the first experiments in decentralization in non-conformist areas, the socialist theoreticians place before themselves the perspective of outstripping living standards in the west, forgetting that the drive for these artificial standards inevitably postpones the day when there will be minimum control and maximum freedom.

And in the underdeveloped or developing world, which covers some two-thirds of the earth's surface, the same kind of psychosis grips the planners. They, too, speak of the day when we will have made up the leeway of centuries and matched the "input" and "output" targets of advanced economies. In the process, there is a marked tendency to emulate the organizational force of both capitalist and socialist society in the private and public sectors—and, also, to accept as civilized all that these forms imply. We are told repeatedly that this is the only way to achieve comfortable, rising standards of living.

India, in a sense, is the perfect example of the folly that grips us. A whole people are being persuaded to turn their back on a tradition which emphasizes that the simple, uncomplicated, full life, which abhors ostentation and advertisement, is the essence of the good life. This tradition, even though hidden by layers of inherited feudal pageantry, is alive among the ordinary people still uncorrupted by the values of the urbanized west. They do not yearn for homes which look awesome palaces. They do not want furnishings of brocade and velvet or chandeliers hanging from the ceilings. Nor are they inspired by the "people's car" or the Cadillac. They can as yet be convinced that there is more comfort in the compact, carefully furnished home, in efficient public transport services, in functional schools, colleges and offices, in the simple, uncomplicated life. But it will not be for long judging from the speed at which the concepts of advanced industrial societies are penetrating the Indian countryside.

The Indian tradition is important, for it may help us to move nearer to the elusive ideal of minimum control and maximum freedom. The staggering waste involved in building up inflated standards, comparable to those prevailing in the U.S.A., can be avoided by projecting the Indian tradition of the simple, full life as something to be desired. Success in this would create a sizable surplus for investment in social and welfare services. In other words, it would not be necessary in terms of India's mounting population, to produce double of what the U.S.A. produces to achieve U.S. standards of living in this country. Nor would it be necessary to give birth to concrete jungles, all-powerful bureaucracies, the kind of development which makes man the victim of his own creations.

Two dangers are to be avoided in the attempt to correct the tendency to repeat the pattern of western industrial societies in India. The first is the danger of getting involved in revivalist nonsense about preserving a peasant-type economy. The second is the danger of trying to impose austerity concepts on the plea that they are necessary for future prosperity. The only way to ensure against these dangers is to embody the values of what I would like to describe as an "integrated society" in the perspective of our economic planning. This is not as easy as it sounds and is not merely confined to emphasizing the need for small-scale industries and decentralization as is so common in our country. It requires a radical reassessment of our borrowed ideas on planning and development. The thought process behind the concept of an integrated society is based on several fundamental ideas.

The yawning, seemingly unbridgeable gulf, between the town and the village in India, must be bridged. How is this to be done?

If we allow the capital goods and consumer good industry to develop where a ready-made technical base already exists, we will have more rapid development, but only in certain areas where industry is already concentrated. The big towns will grow bigger. The villages will remain more or less where they are— in another age. The gulf will become a chasm. Can this industrial development, so essential to a prosperous agriculture, be more evenly spread over the country? The only way is to decentralize, by conscious policy decision, a labour-intensive consumer goods industry. Let the things of daily usage be produced in the rural areas, for, as we shall see, it is here that the demand of tomorrow will build. The already developed industrial areas, and perhaps others, must be reserved for capital goods production—and this, too, should be capital-intensive rather than labour intensive. Light industry, servicing both the consumer goods and capital goods industry, should be so placed as to be available to both.

Of course, any such development is ruled out if agriculture does not develop along new lines. The only way to make land yield much more than it does today is to urge the "garden approach" to land. The Chinese and Japanese farmers have many excellent examples to offer of what can be achieved. But, and this is important, the farmer who is expected to develop the gardeners intensive care for his land must own his land. A strict definition of self-cultivation will have to be evolved to begin with. Then arrangements must be made to provide the essentials of intensive cultivation—an adequate supply of water, selected seed and fertilizer, and also the scientific support to agriculture so sadly lacking today. The surplus from the land will create the surplus for industrialization, particularly of the decentralized consumer goods industry which could be cooperatively run by the farmers and their families in their spare time.

The decentralization or regionalization of the consumer goods industry in rapidly prospering rural areas will inevitably expose these areas to the impact of the technological revolution, absorb surplus labour power, mobilize traditional skills and prevent the growth of monopolies in this particular sector. Indeed, a conscious effort should be made to push development in this direction. Till now, pious platitudes have been in fashion, platitudes which seek to create an artificial Gandhian legend. To do this, the State will have to become active, encouraging and aiding the establishment of decentralized, cooperatively run consumer goods industries. And, of course, the State will open roads and railways to probe the subcontinent, to create a national market for the goods produced.

Clearly, in an integrated society, the State will hold the "commanding heights" in national economy. It will control the capital goods industry which feeds all other industrial development. It will through its services make possible intensive cultivation in the countryside. It will also actively encourage the cooperative structure in the decentralized consumer goods industry and the light industry. But, and this is important, the State will have its role clearly demarcated for a fixed numbers of years, as also its interventionary power within the cooperative sector. Changing conditions may force changes in this role when the reviewing is done by democratic assembly. It is only possible to speak at the moment in terms of general perspectives. The details will require careful working out against the background of a social structure which does not seek the usual standards of living of so-called advanced societies. This aspect should never be forgotten.

And throughout the transitions from one level to another, the creative fields, and the media of mass communication, will need to be entrusted to competing and opposed cooperatives of workers in these fields. Some such structure might still achieve a working fusion between the concepts of freedom and planning.

This essay in "thinking aloud" is merely designed to show that unless we as a nation begin to apply our minds to the solution of problems which have overwhelmed more experienced and advanced societies, we will merely be treading the beaten path, refusing to learn from the experience of others, and knowing not why. Surely, to achieve an integrated society in this rather complicated frustrating age, is the dream of all. What then prevents them from giving shape to the dream? Perhaps, this belated effort towards an integrated society may yet bring within our grasp the ideal of minimum control and maximum freedom!

15

Social and Distributive Justice*

If I were asked to summarize the quest for social and distributive justice during the last twenty-five years, I would say that we forgot Gandhi even as power was transferred. We forgot his emphasis on tackling problems from the base upwards, his assertion of the simple life as the good life. We are now rediscovering him even as we realize that our theories about building a just society on a mixed economy were unrealistic and doomed to failure. On this twenty-fifth anniversary of our freedom we are deeply troubled by the multitude of social problems that our kind of development has spawned. We now know for sure that we must take the correction. We have developed enormously, but our society remains deeply divided. The terribly rich and the terribly poor continue to live side by side. As consciousness grows, the cry rises for an end to this tragic state of affairs. We wonder how to plan the change. Hence the interest in the experience of people other than Anglo-Saxon, in the rebel thinking of fundamentalist political philosophers challenging the growth models which create alienation among peoples and between peoples, and in Gandhi's thought, thought that, incidentally, precedes the latter-day thoughts of Mao Tse-tung and is proving immensely relevant as India looks for correctives.

This is not to suggest that political leadership and parliamentary practise have worked against the current of social and

*A talk in the National Programme of All-India Radio, January 1975.

distributive justice. Quite the contrary. Indeed, one of the remarkable facts of these last twenty-five years has been the heavy stress on egalitarianism and the need to solve the problems of the poor. Our whole political development is punctuated with these battles. Jawaharlal Nehru, Lal Bahadur Shastri, Indira Gandhi lost no opportunity at Prime Minister level to present themselves as the messiahs of egalitarianism.

Take the record. I do not think anyone would controvert the statement that a great deal of time was taken during these twenty-five years to sponsor legislation designed to push the benefits of growth to the poorer sections of society. Rules and regulations, procedures and controls, even institutions were built up to prevent a runaway money-making spree by the rich, by those who possessed, or had the wherewithal to possess, the means of production. A veritable jungle of restraints was carefully nurtured to curb luxury living. Down-trodden castes, and threatened tribal people, were given special protection and weightage to lift them to some level of competitive relevance. The landless were sought to be salvaged through numerous complex laws aimed at re-distributing land and reforming systems of tenure. Income, inheritance, wealth and gift taxes were interlocked in the belief that they would prevent the amassing of fortunes upon which class power is built. Corporate laws, monopoly laws, commissions, committees, and what have you, dominate the Indian political landscape—a reminder that we are wedded to social and distributive justice.

But, and here's the rub, despite all this effort statistics tell us a story which is quite different. Document upon document— official and unofficial—highlights the plight of the poor, the 250 million surviving on a diet terribly deficient in calories. Document upon document, unchallenged, unassailed, tells us that the restraining controls have been subverted, have made the rich richer on captive markets. Statistics are never accurate, but they cannot be all that wrong. We have to face the truth. We have not brought about the transformation we sought in the life of our people these twenty-five eventful years.

The apologists are many—and of different hues. Some point in self-satisfaction to what has been done, claiming that 25 years is a tiny moment in the life of a people. Others warn that too much egalitarianism would have wrecked the rate of growth' dispersed savings and the resources needed for investment in development. A few philosophize about the inevitability of squeezing the poor in the early phases of development, that is, before the fruits really become available. And there are the quiet ones who believe that the Almighty made some for affluence and others for poverty, that it is all in the stars, in the cycle of birth and death.

We have to move beyond the apologists and propagandists. It doesn't require any special study to realize that Indian society is in the throes of a great ferment. An overwhelming majority of over 550 million people cannot any longer tolerate their abject condition. The realization is also general that, with the best will in the world for "mass welfare," every policy decision seems somehow to serve the interests of the well-to-do sections. This is a specific feature of our annual growth rate of some 3.5 to 4 per cent during the planning period. We cannot but focus on the static social structure as destructive of every egalitarian measure.

Let us take as a starting point the assertion of certain political and social observers that India continues to remain perhaps the most inegalitarian society in the world. This is an exaggeration. But it will help us to formulate two sharp questions. Why have we failed to make an impact on poverty over 25 years? And what do we have to do to make this impact?

Many answers will be provided by the first question. It is one of those areas where everyone who thinks has a theory. However, I cannot wander. I do not have the time. I must zero in on the septic focus. At this moment in our history when the tiny percentage of rich are articulate, organized and commanding the levers of powers, and when the poor and desperately poor are scattered and dispersed, divided and confused, without thrust or thought, it is only natural that every legislation designed to ensure social and distributive justice is easily subverted through money, through influence and through legal exercises. This is what has been happening, and political leadership has not been sufficiently oriented to a mass line to work out a follow-up or follow-through capable of rising above the subversion. Political workers at the grassroots have never been sufficiently motivated to ensure that legislative action is matched by strict implementation. There has been no disciplined mobilization of the people to assert their legal rights, only anarchic, haphazard agitation by politicians on the make.

Let me elaborate this further. Nations rising to freedom seek self-reliant, sovereign economic and political power. This gives them the muscle to extricate from the clutches of other more powerful, developed national systems with whom they must inevitably deal. At the same time, there can be no such self-reliant, sovereign assertion without a major effort to lift the people from their wretched living conditions to some level of dignity. Both concepts were inter-locked in the thinking of those who planned the growth of free India, but there was a trend to concentrate on the problems of self-reliance and sovereignty to the neglect of the problem of life and living at the vast, multi-millioned base that is India. Now we are launched upon the correction—with a vengeance.

This brings me to the second question I had raised earlier. What should we do? And here a warning is necessary. We are in danger of repeating the old mistakes. We continue to project bigger doses of egalitarian legislation in a society based on inequalities. In such a situation, as always, every kind of loophole is found to help the rich remain rich or become richer. Indeed, when the loopholes are sought to be plugged, corruption on a wide scale is resorted to. We must face this central contradiction of our situation and resolve it—that is, if we genuinely want social and distributive justice.

How does one go about it? Some suggest that a careful organization of the price system could gradually destroy the gulfs and usher in a socialist society. Others argue that consumption limits can be fixed to prevent a few battening on the many. I am afraid these theories beg the question. I can only see one possible corrective. Social ownership of the means of production has to be steadily extended until the power of private wealth to subvert social and distributive justice is broken. This does not mean total social control immediately. Control certainly of a kind which makes it impossible to subvert policies vital to social and distributive justice. We have been moving in this direction. But the trouble is that wherever social ownership has been applied, the economic result has been far from promising.

In other words, the performance of the public sector has to undergo far-ranging improvement before social ownership can really be pressed. To do so with our present outmoded management, production and marketing would be to invite economic setbacks—at least, that is the fear among those who are not prepared to trust to luck. The hold-ups in steel production cost us some 200 crores last year—the import bill on steel. The run-down for our electric system will create another huge bill. And so on in heavy engineering, in fertilizers etc.

For those who believe in economic growth which impacts the life of the mass of the people, the central task is to demand a public sector management which is comparable to the best. At the same time, the working force of the public sector will have to show exemplary discipline. To see it any other way would be to accept a continuing sabotage of the economy through corrupt and cynical management, through indiscipline and disruption at production points and through meaningless violence and anarchy. In such a state of affairs there's little prospect of success for the efforts being made to establish a society of equals.

I could have spoken a great deal about promises and failures in the area of social and distributive justice. That would have been an awful waste of limited time. In the final analysis we must get to grips with the core problem—that wealth in the key sectors should be produced and distributed under social control. It is here that the critical distortion takes place in our policies. This simple statement embraces many theories, ideas and concepts. We have to find a mix that works, a mix that is aware of Indian realities, but is designed to strengthen the thrust for social and distributive justice. If in the key sectors we can establish social control, manage effectively, and prevent the disruption of production, we would have taken the first step to end poverty. We used to speak about the State commanding the heights of the economy. In practice, the private sector commanded the public sector. In other words, the gap between profession and practise must be bridged. And when it's done, we will be poised to work out a mass line—the production of goods to meet the essential needs of the mass of the people, the organization of mass housing and mass transport as against individual homes and private cars, the creation of an educational and training system which prepares the mass of the people to be more productive, for the strength of our people is in their numbers. This is about the toughest job on hand for those who build parliamentary democracy in our land. Tough. Challenging. Exciting. An agenda for the next twenty-five years.

16

The Mass Line

After surviving many economic and political crises, we are
celebrating the completion of twenty-five years of our democratic Republic. For a people brought up to believe that economic growth consolidates democratic institutions, this anniversary
should help us realize that such simplistic and easy equations
have little relevance; indeed, in social history, very often the
opposite is true.

In India, we now realize that the complexities of continental
politics and continental growth patterns become more forbidding as we develop. Each solution generates a new set of problems. The mounting aspirations of the people also create a new
quality of pressure on policy making. There can be no going
back to the "good old days." But the complacency which once
characterized our attitudes has now been replaced by an exag-
gerated apprehension. This is natural. The failure to anticipate
difficulties has heightened anxieties.

What is remarkable is that the democratic system has survived,
despite a generally status quo economic situation. If literacy
percentages are up, the actual number of illiterates has increased. If development has taken place, poverty in quantum has
increased. If many more thousands throng the universities, they
come out less equipped to earn a living than ever before. "God
must be Indian!" exclaim startled visitors. The thought is excit-

*From *Seminar*, 160, December 1972.

ed by the extraordinary contrasts which exist side by side in India, contrasts which in any other country would spark anger and violence. But we shouldn't imagine that anger and violence can be forever quietened by the chanting of populist ministerial slogans.

Obviously, the Indian is ideal material for the "hastening slowly" philosophy which underpins any political system in which dissent is embodied and cherished. However, the supposedly wise and patient Indian cannot be expected to tolerate a status quo situation in perpetuity. Indeed we are today witnessing the end of the first phase in our democratic experiment.

The status quo situation, in which the broad picture of affluence and poverty remained relatively unaffected by growth, has been stirred up by the recent shifts in power alignments and personalities within the amorphous Congress Party which continues to straddle the country. Quite clearly, a new economic balance will have to be found to underpin the new democratic stirring in the system—and it has to be found fairly soon, considering the explosive tensions which are building at the level of the mass base under the outward confidence and calm generated by the successful solution of the Bangladesh problem.

So far, the debate on economic-political issues, more intense than it has ever been during these years of freedom, is confined to a traditional kind of clash between the ideologies of the Right and Left. We continue to excite ourselves over the relative merits of the private and public sectors, over the burdens of direct and indirect taxation, over licensing policies and their relation to monopoly, productivity and paralysis, and over a host of other related issues. We continue to imagine that the confrontations along which we discuss are designed to resolve the problems of poverty now threatening the stability of our democratic system. Nothing could be further from the truth. This is emphasized by the limited surveys so far undertaken of the living conditions of our people. In other words, both Left and Right continue to assume a framework which is conservative in time and foreign in concept.

If this democratic continental federation, with its many and varied communities and aspirations, is to survive, the growth model by which we have experimented these last twenty-five years has to be changed. Under the present approach, every advance throws up a multitude of new crises, crises which will overwhelm our democratic system if we do not change the quality of our development, or the value system which designs the priorities that structure our society.

In other words, Indian democracy demands a growth model which ensures substantial changes in the basic living conditions of the mass of our people within their life time. To continue as at present, with the middle classes in the saddle, is to place too much faith in transmigration as the promise of fulfilment for the people! Our people want their life to change in their life-time, and if it cannot be done in a democracy they will seek other ways.

We have always assumed that such an objective is woolly and unrealistic. But it is? Certainly, if we continue in intellectual subservience to the borrowed concepts which we have proclaimed as sacrosanct in our twenty-five years of freedom. Certainly not, if we take courage and attempt an overhaul of objectives and the steps needed to achieve those objectives.

While we are reviewing the critical question of a new economic balance for our democratic transition, we should always keep in mind that the answer has to be found within the context of Indian experience at the base of the economic structure: the peasant, the craftsman, the worker, the student, the unemployed, the homeless and the hungry. To formulate the answer in rigid rightist or leftist frames, as is the prevailing style, could be unrealistic; the polarization inherent in such postures would be a threat to the unity of this multi-cultural, multi-national subcontinent. And, yet, both projected stereotyped solutions fail to relate to the actual reality.

Then, again, the lesson of Bangladesh is not lost upon us. To be relevant, the political ideology has to be sufficiently sensitive to federal pressures even as it is dynamic, thrusting and mass-oriented. Anything less would be dismissed by even our own tolerant and patient people as a hoax devised to serve the more fortunate regions or individuals in our society.

How is it possible to create a political philosophy sufficiently dynamic-revolutionary in concept—to guarantee the stability of our democracy?

The way to go about this enormous task is to state categorically that every theory and plan will be tested on the basis of what it is likely to do for the mass of the people. Mahatma Gandhi had such a "talisman." Our present leadership needs to devise one: something in the nature of "a mass line." It is not a populist slogan. It bases itself on solving the problems of the people at the grassroots, within a value system which emphasizes a simple and just social order, hastening slowly but surely, testing achievments at the mass base, avoiding the pitfalls experienced by more advanced societies.

I believe it is possible to achieve this critical correction in our thought and action if we attempt it now—that is before the wrong values of the wasteful, affluent society have taken over. We talk glibly about bridging the many gulfs between our people, and of the need to be egalitarian in outlook and policy, but we do everything possible through planning processes, rules and regulations, and value systems, to increase the gulfs. Twenty-five years of freedom have not seen any improvement in this economic-social stratification. Instead, we are creating amongst our young, dreams of affluence which can neither be fulfilled in our economic conditions, nor are worthy of fulfilment. The craving for a consumer society is growing among, believe it or not, both Left and Right—and so is the frustration.

The leadership continues to flourish slogans which confuse the goals and make them recede further and further away from the horizon. And now a growing impatience which creates cynicism about policy pronouncements on "socialism," generates bitterness and anger which easily build to violence. The shadow of Calcutta haunts many an Indian city.

The seventies will be dominated by the debate around this central issue of how to plan the future. No party can afford to neglect it. No party can any longer run for remedies to economic models which have little relevance to Indian continental realities. All parties will be compelled to exercise themselves over the evolution of a new growth model which can sustain our federal democratic system.

I am of the opinion that the model must be based upon a mass line. And a mass line, to make an impact on today's situation, must cut across the usual polarizing slogans of the Right and Left and focus on the key problems of the people. The "base" should become the centre of concern. In this manner, the mass line becomes the ideology of a dynamic, new formation.

It is the area of common national agreement and it is enough
to keep us busy for a long time.

What are the objectives of such a mass line?

(*a*) Control and stabilize the prices of the necessities of mass
consumption without which peace on the production front
will break down.

(*b*) Try and rid the Indian psyche of the idea of a job
being something fixed, confined and constant. Create jobs on
a mass scale for engineers, students and the landless through
land armies and rural works programmes, which will build
immense capital resources throughout the land, lessen the
gap between town and village, provide a visible example of
action-oriented programmes and socially transform human
relationships in town and village.

(*c*) Give priority to an interlinked system for mass housing
and mass transport at the expense of private housing and
private transport. No private homes for the more affluent
until the poor have been housed, no "small" cars until mass
transport needs are fulfilled. Slogans of "mass housing" have
not provided a roof for our people in the last 25 years; small
cars have not lessened the trauma of people going to work as
the cities expand to unmanageable proportions.

(*d*) Spell out the perspectives for mass literacy and competence in various technical skills in relations to the capacities
demanded by the developing situation. Education has to be
pulled out of the universities to serve the real needs of our
people at the base. A radically different approach to education
has to be evolved, gathering the new communication power
of radio and TV.

(*e*) Break the vicious neglect of the village, its life and productivity by bringing more modern technology to the village
craftsman and helping him to create a link with the national
market. His skill has to be considered a national resource,
to be helped and exploited. Japan's experience is vital in this.
Magnetic points have to be established in the rural areas to
halt the aimless migration into the towns.

(*f*) Democratize and decentralize the present administrative system by making it result-oriented, so that the specialized experience available outside the system can be utilized with

proper delegation at critical points instead of the present generalist, hierarchical, bureaucratic cadres rooted in preserving the status quo. Wider participation with responsibility should be the effort.

The moment the bare outlines of a mass line to underpin our democracy are sketched, so many of the priorities by which we have lived these twenty-five years are brought into question, from how much steel we require to how many graduates, how many committees, how many cars and so on. Then political and economic reforms come under disciplined scrutiny. The mass line becomes the motivator of policies and perspectives. An experimental application of this approach to a narrow area of development immediately throws up a new frame of operation.

I believe it is possible to achieve the necessary corrections in our policies and implementations through democratic, peaceful sanctions if we begin to stir ourselves out of the old grooves. And a critical point of stirring is obviously the Planning Commission. It must become a major weapon in the structural transformation of India. It is here that the development framework for the next 25 years must immediately be detailed, as also the system of implementation at various levels. Such an objective demands an immediate, drastic overhaul of the Commission. The economics of democracy in a developing society must be understood more creatively at Yojna Bhavan. No longer can we rest content with injecting radicalism into the content of planning without drastically altering the frame of planning. This has been our gravest error. What is attempted so far is nowhere near enough.

Our democracy is shaping very differently from the models in the West with which we have been familiar. Our economic system, too, must find its roots in its own soil and throw up concepts which make sense in our social setting. Political and economic leadership must combine to attack the problem of poverty and despair in India without cant and double talk.

In other words, the essential elements of a developing society have already been nurtured. Only a catalyst is needed to crystallize a stable democracy. And that is a mass line . . .

17

Communications and Changing Values*

Public relations. Relations with the public. Communications. Changing values. Responsible citizenship. We bandy words about with the ease of modern princelings. We must be careful. We must move warily. Or else we will be talking to ourselves.

We know a great deal about modern communications, and what they can do: batter, bruise, mould, modify, confuse and motivate masses of people. This revolution in communications is now entering our country with an extraordinary impact. If Mahatma Gandhi and Jawaharlal Nehru had physically to visit the constituency that is India to get the message of revolt and freedom across, their successors have only to use the radio intelligently. The transistor and the battery have linked the most distant hamlet to the centres of political power. Electronic technology is going to see great expansion, precise sharpening and careful streamlining in the years ahead—oil or no oil—and we are going to face immense problems of a kind qualitatively different to those of the past.

We will soon be witnessing the electronic death of a traditional system of communication which permitted a single individual to raise his voice of support or protest, of confusion

*Address to the Fourth All-India Public Relations Conference, Bombay, January 1974.

or dissent. Modern technology places vast and basically un-controllable power in the hands of governments, corporations, political parties, politicians and "operators" (for want of a better phrase) to direct thinking, to push people from one point of view to another. Interestingly, so many of us who are deeply worried by this fact of mass communications technology, its scale and expense, are at the same time working overtime to improve the technology, to make its impact on mass thinking more and more effective. And what is mass thinking? Values, of course, changing values, if you wish—but let us not forget who is changing the changing values.

Whose values are we concerned with? Mine? Yours? The talent-ed semi-literates who dominate the mass media because their mental equipment is uncluttered with doubts, anxieties and question marks? My people who live in degradation and squalor? Whose values, or changing values, are we talking about? This needling, for that is what it is, is necessary even when we range over the apparently innocuous subject of "responsible citizenship."

The first point I want to make is that we can no longer talk within old frameworks. Responsible citizenship is not a matter of supporting the norms of law and order, of balanced debate, of the institutions of the status quo. Quite contrary positions are possible within a responsible citizen. He could dedicate himself to the destruction of the entire iniquitous structure—and win mass acclaim. Similarly, changing values are not vague genera-lizations about violence, about generation gaps, the breakdown of the religious hold, free sex and amorality, the justification of wrong-doing. Communications have to approach the business of values and change and in the context of those values which make the future and those which destroy it. This means comprehend-ing the totality of change—industrial, scientific, technological—or what we continue to describe vaguely as economic, political and social. In other words, a communicator, to intervene effectively, will have to possess more than the usual superficial equipment for "soft-sell" and "hard-sell," whatever the product. Indeed, he will have to make the effort to become a philosopher for the future. He cannot live in the cliches of the past and obsessions of the present.

I am making this point about the framework of thinking because so much of communication, is alas, merely a device to preserve the status quo—or to ginger it up. It has become over the years a prostituted profession, and so many of the theoreticians it has thrown up are little more than cynical motivators. I am glad we are meeting in India to discuss this problem. We are part of a population of 575 millions. Probably, we will be 1000 million by the year 2000. It's a raw challenge. We can't run away from it merely by mounting the cliches and obsessions of a Greek past and an Anglo-Saxon present. We forget the slaves of olden days. We forget the Vietnam of today. Empty postures look emptier in such an environment. And not far away is China, even more oppressed by population and politics, hoping that its new collectivist frameworks will survive, become a model. Asia will have to come to grips with these realities—and the world, too, for the surging anger that can spill over from these regions could hold the world in a terrible trauma. Significantly, this same Asia gave us in our life time two extraordinary persons. Gandhi. Mao. Very different, very contrary—and yet, speaking a language very similar if you see the content of their thought in values, changing values. And, yet, how many of us communicators have any understanding of these two "phenomena." After all, between them, they moved a majority of mankind—and without advertising budgets.

It is against this backdrop of actuality, an area over which we could debate for months, that we have to begin probing our role as communicators, whatever the technical field of our specification. Looking at it in this way, there is too much to talk about. So ... we'll have to confine ourselves to the key questions, leaving the answers to develop as we cogitate upon them.

For example, do we have any idea whatsoever about where we think our civilization is headed? I say "our" because it is the first civilization with a faint glimmer of universality.

Would you agree that as the world shrinks, time-wise and space-wise, and the revolution of science and technology marches on with its fantastic built-in effect of widening the gap between advanced and backward, a cultural imperialism of the affluent is crystallizing as a major threat to all value systems? Indeed, even tourism can and has become such a threat. Do I need to explain?

We speak so much about the liberation of man—a fact sym-

bolized by the non-conformist thrust of youth in most lands—but
do you think this movement in its varied forms can achieve any
lasting social transformations without a conscious projection of
new value systems and new yardsticks for measuring man's
progress?

Let me make it more precise. Our planet is in trouble. Some
of us—a tiny minority—consume too much. The overwhelming
majority do not, are denied, frustrated. Somehow, we have to
find and propagate the civilized level of consumption. How do
we go about it? Discipline the affluent, both nationally and
internationally? Establish not minimums of consumption, as we
do, but *maxima* beyond which all is waste? Yes, challenge upon
challenge faces the communicator. Do you think we should
assault the standard of living—redefine it, restructure it, refresh
it, convince the people that there is a point beyond which consumption becomes self-destructive? Is it possible? Have we tried
it? And shouldn't we begin with those who are already over-
consuming? That's us, sitting here in this quite unnecessary
luxury.

I hope I am making myself understood. We are communicators. We are without a philosophy for this crisis engulfing the
second half of the twentieth century. Every step we take will hit
us first. And yet we have to take it if we wish to remain relevant.
The moment of choice is upon us. We ignore it at our peril.

Increasingly the charge is levelled that the mass media—and
creative workers—are destroying the moral fibre of our society
by preaching and depicting violence and pornography on a scale
never attempted before. This is almost inevitable because we
fear to present the truth—that the wasteful consumer society is
a deadly menace to those enjoying it and to those unfortunates
who would aspire to it. I say "fear to present the truth," because
the truth is being captured in creative work, but it is not market-
ed. Ask the most enlightened in any field of creativity and they
will confirm this sordid fact. We are being brain-washed even
as we shout against brain-washing. What we objectively need is
a brain-cleaning. Willy nilly, communicators have become the
engineers of the human soul. This is the revolution in communications technologies of the last quarter century. But how do we
go about our jobs. Take the present job. Responsible citizenship, and the values which we must change to make way for

responsibility. Do we leave it to the present anarchy of ideas to determine the direction of developments, the anarchy which is dominated by the wretched figure of the corrupt and cynical politician—yes, from Washington to Paris to Moscow to Delhi to Manila to Tokyo? Or do we define more meaningful objectives and battle for wider and wider acceptance of these tasks? This is the central question we must ask ourselves, individually and collectively, and proceed to influence whatever piddling job we are working at. After all, so many puddles make the stream, the torrent, the spreading river, the Ganga.

Admittedly, communicators work under tremendous constraints—for the power of communication to make and unmake reputations, policies, operations, arrangements and perspectives in every field is now widely understood. But communicators cannot be servitors. This is easily said. So many of us complain bitterly about the pressures on us, but are we not in fact guilty of surrendering to pressures too easily? In my personal experience, I have been horrified at the way in which the dignity and individuality of the communicators, the creative experimenter and the crazy dissenter, is allowed to be bruised by so-called clients and even by colleagues who prattle a great deal about these principles. This shameless let-down by the professionals themselves has to be focussed on before these can be any crystallization or confrontation on any front.

If we go on as we are, we might, unconsciously, push ourselves and our complexities into an authoritarian system of political management. The revolution of science and technology, even as it liberates humankind from the thraldom of sweated labour, creates propulsions in the direction of authoritarianism. The modern state, whether capitalist, communist or mixed, demands conformism to the broad values of whatever status quo is prevailing. The state uses the revolution of science and technology, born out of dissent and conflict, to this barren end. We, the communicators, have therefore to play two roles within one. Communicate and articulate. These roles can be conflicting. We have to be wary as to which role is demanded of us and at what point. Let us always remember that responsible citizenship is not status quoist. It demands responsiveness to the thrust of society into the future. In other words, communications must increasingly be opened up to the citizenry, the good citizens who have a great deal to say on the activities of governments, corporations, political parties, politicians and "operators." Popular participation in communications, participatory communications, will become in the years ahead a sign of the health of a society. Through such participation, yet to be organized without manipulation, we will comprehend the emerging values, the changing values, and help speed the process of change in the interests of a viable future.

Forgive me for linking public relations, responsible citizenship, communications and changing values in so tortuous a manner. Life is, after all, getting terribly complicated . . .

18

Contradictions in Co-existence[*]

Co-existence is about the most over-used word in the vocabulary of international politics. Indeed, if it is now in danger of
being consigned to the store-house of cliches, the fault is ours.
Over the years, it has become an invocation rather than a
catalyst to correct the imbalances in the relationships among us
who inhabit this planet. I say this because co-existence between
unequals must remain tentative, uncertain, dictated only by
fears of many descriptions, including nuclear suicide. To move
boldly towards a more solid detente is our task—and it is only
possible if we cut through vague generalities in an attempt to
isolate the causes of our failure to make the concept a real and
living faith.

We speak with passion in support of co-existence here and
elsewhere, but we tend to slur over our commitments to a
variety of political, economic and social policies or concepts
which polarize our human society, create the very tensions and
divisions that transform co-existence into an argument for the
perpetuation of a status quo which at least two-thirds of mankind—the developing world—rejects. This dichotomy in our
attitude to building the structure of peace on earth devalues
all our efforts and will inevitably bring it into contempt.

I am not suggesting that immediate or total solutions are
possible to the problems which divide mankind, but I do feel

[*]Intervention at "Pacem in Terris II," Geneva, 1967.

that we cannot narrow down the threat to co-existence as competition among nations or ideologies which manifests itself in
military intervention or military confrontation. Admittedly, the
failure of the political-military front has to be tackled with all
the energy and wisdom we possess, for this failure can shatter
the basis of our survival. But we would be abandoning our responsibilities if we ignored those other trends in our affairs which
are sharpening polarization between nations and continents.

The world and its affairs, Jawaharlal Nehru used to say, take
on a different aspect depending on whether you view them from
Washington or London or Paris or Moscow or Peking or Tokyo
or Delhi. The trouble is that in the not-so-distant past we looked at them from London and Paris. Now, we are considering
them from Washington and Moscow. In a gathering like this
we must take a world view of the world. And what do we see?

If it is military intervention and military confrontation, now
largely focussed in the regions of the developing world, the
single fact which stands out is the polarization that is being
fed not only within a nation but between the nations of the
disturbed region. The people of Viet Nam have known no peace
for twenty years, not because they have so willed, but because
their territory is chosen to be the point where the power of rival
hegemonists is to be demonstrated. The polarization, dictated
by the external powers, vitiates the dialogue in Asia and
prevents the movement towards a solution of many outstanding
problems.

The aggressive presence of external powers in any region,
their dogged search for spheres of influence, and the fact that
local elites are often persuaded that their interests coincide with
the interests of the interventionists destroys sovereign expression and creates an atmosphere of explosive frustration whatever the rights and wrongs of the issue in dispute. In all honesty
we must face this reality and attempt to explore the answers.
The external powers, we will discover, have to withdraw if political health is to return. How many of us are prepared to subscribe to this doctrine?

Similarly, when we study the pattern of economic growth in
our world today, we are startled by the warning that statistics
give. The deep and developing contradiction in the distribution
of economic rosources and population is well-known, but not

nearly so widely publicized is the proven thesis that the policies of the past two decades of so-called decolonization have further impoverished the poverty stricken majority of mankind. Today, 89 per cent of the world's income, 85.5 per cent of its gold and foreign currency, 93.3 per cent of its steel, 89.2 per cent of its pig iron output, and 72 per cent of its power production are concentrated in thirty countries. Thirty years ago, the developing countries were still exporting 11 million tons of grain a year; but ten years later they were importing cereals—and those imports rose to 29 million tons in 1964. Between 1950 and 1962 the average national income per person increased to $1044 a year in the industrially advanced countries of the west, and dropped to $ 67 in the developing world. Trade practices, price fixing and other unequal impositions have brought about this result. Here is a polarization at the economic level which can make nonsense of co-existence in the years ahead.

Significantly, the UN-sponsored Development Decade, now coming to an end, is one of the massive failures of our time. However, in the literature on co-existence, the lessons of this decade and the implications of the policies adopted by the rich nations against the poor nations are not even mentioned. We are, indeed, being persuaded to divorce economics from politics.

And when the questioning becomes too intense, reference is made to the aid given by the advanced countries. Apart from the rather limited nature of this operation, and its frequent connection with the interventionist activity of the external powers, the statistics again startle the researcher. In Latin America, for example, according to the Secretary-General of the World Trade Conference, the inflow of foreign capital amounts to 9,600 million dollars. This exercise in aid is being repeated in many parts of our world.

The very momentum of unequal growth sharpens the contrasts in every field, particularly in the scientific and technological. These in turn nourish the polarization at social and cultural levels. The problems of racial tension are to be considered in this context, and are very much part of the total approach we must attempt to popularize if co-existence is to become a meaningful weapon.

I have stressed the contradictions in our attitudes because I do not believe it is possible to destroy war as a method of solving disputes unless we lay the groundwork for peace. The advanced nations will continue to spend 180,000 million dollars on armaments so long as they rest content to expend only 8000 million dollars on dissolving the tensions which generate wars. There is no way out, except through a radical reversal of accepted priorities.

19

After the China Clash*

New words are creeping into the everyday speech of India, un-
familiar words which have a violent ring and that stale taste of
war. Irregular forces . . . defence in depth . . . limited deterrent
. . . commandos and guerillas . . . air umbrella . . . mobilization . . . conscription . . . missiles, mortars, automatics . . .
air raid precautions . . . and so it goes on as more and more
people in our country become actively interested in the effective
organization of armies, air forces and navies.

These words and expressions were not relevant to the Indian
context until the collision with China in the Himalayas. Now,
they are likely to stay. For, the Indian mind is sorely troubled
by the cynical aggression of China's armies and the violation of
generally accepted and peaceful frontiers.

I stress this aspect of the change which is taking place because defence has become an overriding consideration in Indian
policy-making. The recent budget of the Government of India,
embodying a defence expenditure of nearly Rs. 900 crores,
brought this fact into sharp focus. And, judging from the calm
acceptance of the new tax burdens, it looks very much as if
Prime Minister Nehru's call to find the funds not only for increased defence spending but also for a steady rate of economic
growth is being answered.

However, dangerous contradictions can take shape if the

*From a talk to the National Defence College, 1963.

response to the new challenges posed by the Chinese unprovok-
ed attack and unilateral withdrawal is not sober and rational,
based upon a scientific assessment of national and international
trends.

When we look back upon the tortuous story of the Indo-
China border conflict, what do we see? So long as a semi-auto-
nomous Tibet was a buffer between these two States, all was
well. The token presence of Chinese authority, including troops,
did not disturb relations between Peking and Delhi, although it
is true that new tensions began to be felt in the Himalayan
Kingdoms of Sikkim, Bhutan and Nepal which were closely
allied to India.

The Khampa revolt in Tibet, Peking's decision to move into
the region massively, the flight of the Dalai Lama to India and
Delhi's openly expressed disillusionment over China's tough
posturings—all these events in rapid succession destroyed the
basis upon which the friendship and cooperation of Asia's two
most numerous peoples was being built. Whether Peking's Marxist theoreticians acted deliberately or not is another matter.
Suffice it to say that these events sparked a political crisis which
was to have wide repercussions, embracing in its sweep China's
relations with the Soviet Union.

The second point to note is that there can be no understanding of the collision along the Himalayas unless we grasp the
essentials of the Moscow-Peking rift and how it influenced the
actions of India. Ever since the attempt by a Dulles-dominated
US State Department to polarize the situation in South Asia
between communists and anti-communists, the Indian government has assumed non-aligned attitudes. It was also generally
understood that these would be viable so long as the Soviet
Union chose to respect non-alignment—and non-alignment won
this respect with the dethronement of dogmatic Stalinism.

But India's policy-makers failed to assess correctly the strength
of the new-Stalinist trends in neighbouring China which began
to crystallize soon after the Bandung Conference. Jawaharlal
Nehru put his faith in the capacity of the USSR to curb Chinese
adventurism against non-aligned India, a faith which should
have been abandoned when the Chinese invested Tibet and
moved across the Aksai Chin region along the "international
frontier" in Ladakh on India's extreme north, an uninhabited

wasteland which had become important to Peking as a vital and reliable gateway into Tibet.

At that time (between 1954-59), when relations were still cordial, the Indian Government could have negotiated a territory swop to settle the Himalayan border; the Chinese leaders would also most probably have been agreeable. But Jawaharlal Nehru, fearing that a surrender of Aksai Chin would further consolidate Chinese communist power along the now vulnerable Himalayas, and somewhat confident that the Soviet Union could still be relied on to contain and discipline the Chinese leadership, played for time. Indeed, he witheld news of the earlier Chinese incursions from his own people.

It was only when Peking persisted in expanding her claims that the matter was publicly debated and made an issue of further friendship. However, Nehru and his advisers refused to believe that Mao Tse-tung's China would risk war to assert its claim to waste-lands in the Himalayas. This erroneous assessment, shared by the vast majority of thinking India, led to a series of decisions which encouraged Chinese adventurism.

As the Chinese leadership pressed forward with its claims, and mounted a tremendous propaganda barrage throughout the world in support of them, the Indian Government realized that the adventurers would have to be confronted. This decision was taken in the middle of 1961, but the sad fact remained that India was in no way prepared for the confrontation.

Militarily, her forces were ill-equipped and inadequate. Politically, there was danger that the confrontation with China would be used by extreme right wing elements to dislodge the government of Jawaharlal Nehru. Financially, the country could not afford to underwrite the cost of an effective border policy without damaging the economy and its rate of growth, already perilously low. Diplomatically, there was a possibility that a non-aligned India could be pushed into a position of commitment.

Prime Minister Nehru decided that a "demonstration" by India that she would resist encroachments on her territory would have a salutory effect on China, for the belief continued that China would definitely avoid an armed collision with a leader of the non-aligned world. This was the background against which the erroneously named "forward policy" in Ladakh was fashioned.

The purpose of the 'forward policy' was to somehow contest the expanding claims of China as expressed in 1956, and in 1960 to somehow prevent her (without clashes) from taking physical possession of her full 1960 claims, and to somehow prevent her from establishing a viable and easily demarcatable line of control. The policy consisted of establishing tiny pickets supplied from the air, at widely separated points, often behind the continuously advancing Chinese outposts which were linked by highways.

The Indian army, although heavily involved along the Kashmir-Pakistan front and committed to a difficult campaign against the Naga rebels in the east, undertook to implement this forward policy despite logistic problems created by the lack of communications and the heavy strain which would be placed on reserves of equipment and manpower. It was at this time that the Goa action was also ordered—a minor campaign which revealed serious shortages in supply and should have cautioned the government about any further involvements.

The army staff was worried over the manner in which its forces were being fully committed on widely separated fronts and varied terrain without proper thought being given to ensuring equipment and supplies, let alone building essential reserves. Soon after the Goa operation, this sorry state of affairs was openly discussed in Delhi. It was well known that the army staff had detailed the shortage and indicated that the armed forces would we compromised in an emergency if immediate steps were not taken to make good the shortages.

Nobody took these proddings seriously. We were wedded to the idea of demonstrative strength in supersonic fighters, which involved an expensive ground organization when what we required were small arms (to meet the fire power of the Chinese) and tanks (to deter Pakistan from undertaking new adventures). At governmental and parliamentary levels the opinion was general that a non-aligned India faced no real threat and could afford to conserve her resources for economic developments.

Gradually, the army staff became infected by the assessment of the politicians. Chinese activity south of the Karakoram mountains in Ladakh was not seen as a developing engagement. And when Peking moved to break the peace in NEFA in the East, we assumed that this was merely a tactic to make the entire Himalayan border negotiable. The order to "push" the Chinese out was given in the belief that they were unlikely to stage a major clash to obstruct us.

However, later events made clear that Peking had decided to lay a careful trap to justify a massive punitive expedition in the NEFA against the numerically inferior and ill equipped Indian army. Before the Indian army could move to "push" the enemy out of its territory a full-blooded invasion had been launched. The nature and size of the invasion revealed Chinese intentions once and for all, despite their skilful and voluminous propaganda of being the aggrieved party.

The rest of the story is well known. Even as the outlines of a total war began to be sketched between two Asian neighbours, Peking ordered a unilateral cease fire and withdrawal. Quiet again descended along the Himalayas but the peace was a very uncertain one.

During the height of the Chinese invasion, the government of Jawaharlal Nehru, startled by the perfidy of a neighbour who for long had pretended friendship, and under heavy attack from domestic political opponents, moved to ensure the country's defence in the event of a large scale Chinese advance into India. Appeals were addressed to all powers to express their solidarity with India and to aid her defence. The response was immediate from those already committed to the battle against communism; they saw in this situation the opportunity to persuade India to abandon her principled non-aligned stand for something more flexible.

The communist world, already deeply divided by ideological controversies and the tensions over Cuba, preferred silent diplomacy in an attempt to bring sanity to China's adventurist leadership; the Soviet Union it now transpires cut oil supplies to China to make herself understood, for in Moscow there was no doubt that Peking's foolhardy action along the Himalayas was designed to push a politically unstable India into a military commitment with the west and so reduce the concept of non-alignment to a thing of shreds and patches.

Reactions among the non-aligned varied depending on the degree to which they understood the border problems and wanted to intervene. By and large, India had the satisfaction of isolating China diplomatieally, despite brilliant moves by Peking.

But diplomatic victories alone could not provide a sense of security to the Indian people, now that the Himalayas, a traditional barrier to invasion, had been pierced by a powerful neighbour. This traumatic shock could only be cushioned by adequate military insurance for the future, which the Indian Government began to organize. Only the west was prepared to provide it, but at a price. The price was a surrender on Kashmir which was coveted by Pakistan, ally in SEATO and CENTO. This price, India was not prepared to pay, but the need for adequate military insurance also could not be ignored. Involvement at various levels began to take shape.

During the Chinese invasion, the Indian army staff had been refused permission to withdraw the mountain warfare trained and acclimatized divisions held in reserve for the Pakistan front; the Government of India considered that the threat from Pakistan could crystallize at any moment. Then, the army staff sought to get sanction for a plan which would place an armoured deterrent in the plains of the Punjab along the Pakistan frontier and permit a withdrawal of fighting formations from the mountains in the north. This plan was vetoed by the USA and the UK who sought to prevent any strengthening of the Indian army facing Pakistan; tanks and tank spare parts were refused on the spurious plea that they could not be used against the Chinese in the mountains of the north-eastern frontier. India was soon made to realize that massive military aid could only materialize on the basis of a settlement of outstanding problems with Pakistan (meaning, the handing over of strategic Kashmir).

Nevertheless, caught unprepared, the Indian Government was compelled at the most critical moment of invasion to think of a kind of partial military commitment to the west. This semi-commitment, based on a panicky assessment of Chinese intentions, and now sought to be corrected by Prime Minister Nehru, has set in motion a number of trends which might yet embarrass the independence and sovereignty of India.

It is absolutely logical for a non-aligned State, threatened by a neighbour, to obtain military hardware (and even physical support, should this be necessary) in order to defend its independence and sovereignty. Of course, if the attack is launched by irresponsible junior partners in any of the blocs (Britain and

France in Suez, and China in the Himalayas) it is normal in this nuclear enveloped world to expect pressures to mount in both the blocs to insulate the threat. Interestingly enough, this was remarkably well illustrated when non-aligned Egypt and India faced aggression. However, India's leadership, or a major section of it, failed to appreciate the calculations of Prime Minister Nehru, whether short-term or long-term.

The short-term perspective placed before the country by the communist-socialist-liberal wing of political life was to mobilize resources to the maximum to sustain the new defence effort and to preserve the objectives of the economic plans. Any gaps in the effort to maintain the progress of India were to be bridged by foreign aid, military and economic. Unorthodox methods were to be found, particularly in the field of military science, to make both economic growth and a defence build-up possible. At the same time, efforts to evolve a peaceful demarcation of frontiers on the ground were to be intensified.

Prime Minister Nehru, while fully backing this rational approach, did not actively contest those elements within his own government and party who wanted a full commitment to the west; these elements were even permitted to echo the shrieking slogans of the Hindu revivalists and extreme right wingers who demanded nothing less than an all-out shooting war against China, whatever the consequences, nationally or internationally. These lapses laid the basis for pressures which pushed the government of Jawaharlal Nehru into compromising postures on long-term issues.

For example, Britain and the USA, particularly the former, now openly asserted that there was no immediate threat of another invasion and that there could be no long-term military aid for India until a rapproachment with Pakistan was arranged. India's efforts in this direction were turned down by Pakistan. Meanwhile, Britain, seeking close marketing relations with an isolated China, viewed with favour Pakistan's independent efforts to settle with Peking and also considered that support to these efforts would restore her initiatives on the India-Pak subcontinent. The USA was pursuaded to modify her opposition to Pakistan's new "independence" and to increase the pressure on India over Kashmir. Even the dismemberment of north-western and eastern India between China and Pakistan and the internal weaknesses which might result in India would, it was considered, mean one less big power to cope with in the underdeveloped world, and so help correct the balance of world forces!

At the moment, while encouraged to resist Chinese demands, India is given no assurance about the regular flow of military aid. Indeed, long-term military aid, in view of the deadlock in the Kashmir parleys, has been ruled out on the plea that India might use the aid against Pakistan. There is just a slim chance that the immediate commitment to equip five new mountain warfare divisions will be met. The uncertainty is due to the fact that India has refused to permit the USA to establish a permanent nucleus of an "air umbrella," with radar screens running along the Himalayas and a network of serviced airfields across the subcontinent. Prime Minister Nehru would like to see this nucleus established, maintained and serviced by Indian personnel to be made available to supporting air forces should the situation warrant. This view is rejected as "unpractical." The Indian delegations which have been visiting the capitals of the west still hope to mobilize a certain amount of aid to reduce the strain on limited internal resources.

There is, on the other hand, an influential body of official opinion which urges a more active exploration of aid possibilities from the communist countries. It is known that the Soviet Union, publicly pledged to carry out old commitments like the MIG production project, has indicated willingness to assist India in expanding those industrial sectors which are vital to defence; this trend has strengthened as the rift with China has widened. Yugoslavia has made it known that she is prepared to meet Indian orders against local currency. Impressive offers to manufacture arms have come from Czechoslovakia. In the past, communist willingness to aid India has prodded the west, made it more reasonable. This may yet happen on the problems spawned by the emergency in India.

In the course of a brief review, it is not possible to deal with the multitude of trends released by the Chinese invasion and withdrawal. While India has no intention of allowing herself again to be trapped by Peking's extraordinarily flexible diplomacy, backed by armed might, she is determined to build military muscle of the kind which could be nourished by internal resources. The forging of this limited but effective defence is a

difficult task in a political democracy, which takes time to understand the subtleties of the international situation, subtleties
which indicate that when a military engagement between two
countries of the size of India and China develop beyond a
certain stage the world becomes involved.

The task of the present Indian leadership is to demarcate this
stage, to mobilize internal resources for this limited action, to
prepare diplomatically to break a major invasion, to comprehend the likely motivations of Chinese policy during the period
now unfolding, and to sustain a rate of economic growth which
will give viability to the social system which is associated with
the name of Jawaharlal Nehru—a socialist, democratic, secular
system.

Is this mammoth undertaking feasible in a world which is
sharply divided? It is a question that has formed again and
again, not only in India, but in many lands more affluent,
better equipped to answer. In India, we continue to hope that
we will find this answer even though these last few months have
destroyed much of the old confidence.

20

Asian Situation*

Any realistic study of the situation in Asia, particularly the
economic and political, gets inextricably involved with contrary
assessments of the actual strategic objectives of the major external powers—and the resources they are likely to mobilize to
achieve these objectives. More often than not, whether in South-
East Asia or West Asia, it is the external presence in our continent which dictates the dimensions of the challenges and the
kind of responses which have to be fashioned. Those who
attempt, therefore, to turn a blind eye to this uncomfortable fact
will produce theories on security which willy nilly make Asian
interests subservient to those of the advanced nations. Naturally
the objectives and resources of the external powers vary. We
should, however, be concerned in the present period with the
business of locating the common factors which tend to motivate
the several external power centres in their interpretation of
Asian realities—and whether these factors are likely to undergo
any substantial changes as a result of other developing influences.
There are contradictions, tensions and conflicts between these
power centres with the interests of the major centres (the USA
and the USSR) buttressed by junior partners in their respective
regions, but at the same time areas of agreement are emerging
which are of vital concern to Asia and the rest of the developing world.

*From *Seminar* 96; August 1967.

Broadly, the external powers, headed by the USA and the USSR, are acting in unison at various levels, that is if we guage the impact of their nuclear-enveloped policies from the end-results of their initiatives. Despite their different standpoints, they seek:

(*a*) To preserve mutually convenient status quo in Asia based on existing realities of Japan, China and India with the States of South-East Asia and West Asia providing zones of competition where changes in political balance and alignment to the external power centres are reflected;

(*b*) To prevent the purposeful coming together of diverse Asian opinion to project the common interests of a sprawling continent in international organization;

(*c*) To dictate, in one way or another, unequal terms on which economic growth will be aided in the underdeveloped part of Asia, terms which damage or erode the sovereign spirit of free peoples;

(*d*) To deny the bigger States of Asia the possibility of an independent military role on the plea that it is a danger to stability in a particular region and to make this role subservient to the interests of the external powers, thereby securing their economic presence; and

(*e*) To impose norms of political and economic behaviour which in the long run make inter-Asian security dependent on various types of external "protection," including the economic.

The end results of these policies can be seen in the developing polarizations—within Asian nations and between them—at political, economic and military levels. These, in turn, create cultural polarizations. The surface status quo situation is in this manner charged with explosive content. The stability of national governments is threatened and at the same time their security is exposed to grave risks. Polarizations sparked by external powers over whom we have no control create unnecessary and crippling economic-political burdens for developing societies. Not enough attention is being given to this fact of the problem of Asian security. If we are not to become the unthinking victims of the present discernible parallelism of the external powers, often referred to as a "detente" forced by the realities of nuclear confrontation, we have to act with skill. The parallelism is shot through with many contradictions rooted in the transitions which our world is making. We must exploit these contradictions to our advantage—and this demands a conscious effort to break the tendency on our part to see the "detente" exclusively through spectacles provided by the external powers or in isolation from certain significant and developing trends.

For example, the so-called Cultural Revolution in China is usually seen only as an aberration affecting the internal pattern of power, but its ideological impact on the communist world, particularly the Soviet Union, is not studied in depth. Mao Tse-tung's theory of the "continuing revolution" in a socialist society, and his stress on the need at regular intervals to purge communist man of bourgeois infection, may be implemented most strangely, and might end in sudden chaos but we would be blunting our own sensitivity if we were to ignore the backdrop to the "Red Guard" rampage.

The Soviet Union, startled by the uncontrolled and ugly passions of the Maoist strategy which has linked minor and major ideological issues with the traditional power ambitions of an imperial China, cannot afford to be insensitive. The lash of the Cultural Revolution in China will stir thinking in neighbouring lands, including the USSR, whose revolutionary elite is accused of being adrift from its proletarian moorings. To retain its ideological relevance, the Soviet Union will search for the ideological trappings—essentially economic—to reinforce enlightened facets of its presence in the underdeveloped world. The momentum for such a role can only be created from an economic surplus generated from within the Soviet economy or through economic collaboration with a number of highly developed industrialized smaller nations. Significantly, the first steps are already being taken.

Then, again, China is seen only as a military threat, but there is a tendency to play down the potential role she is capable of exerting in the trade and commerce of the underdeveloped world. Such a role is dictated by her self-imposed isolation and the need to import vital industrial inputs through an aggressive highly competitive export programme. The Soviet Union gave China a balanced industrial base—a fact which is slurred over. This base, under careful management, can make her a powerful competitor in several fields, particularly with a ready-made marketing organization of Overseas Chinese.

Japan is seen only in the context provided to us by the external powers—a dynamic industrial workshop which is going to help to underwrite the status quo in Asia for them. But we fail to take serious note of the fears of her policy planners. Japan sees herself at the mercy of an export programme based on the mercurial US market which may, sooner or later, be compelled at the expense of Japanese goods to absorb those of its manufactures which are rejected by a revived Europe. She also does not underestimate the competitive challenge of China in South-East Asia where the memories of militarist Japan's rampage in World War II are not easily forgotten.

Conscious of her predicament, and not without solid economic reasoning, Japan seeks a massive collaboration with the Soviet Union in capital and consumer goods—and she is more than conscious that the new materials of Siberia near at hand would make her even more competitive! Recent events in China make the Soviet Union only too responsive. And there is now the distinct possibility of such collaboration yielding for the Soviet Union a meaningful economic surplus which can be used effectively in the developing world, particularly in South and South-East Asia.

At the other end of disturbed Asia, the Arab nations are presented as manipulatable powers, unreliable allies at war among themselves and now at the mercy of Israel. The story sticks, because the surface scene confirms this superficial analysis. However, in power-political terms, the ferment in the Arab world and the strategic position of this region can only be underestimated at our own cost. Israel is an unfortunate and tragic problem, but the attempt by the external powers to place the guilt of Europe on the Arabs and to exploit Israel in the context of Asian resurgence has to be fought. Again, rational thought is discouraged in the interests of a tense status quo which serves the needs of the external powers.

Much the same pattern unfolds as we study the relationship between India and Pakistan. The calculations of the external powers feed the polarization on the subcontinent without the slightest regard to the disastrous consequences on the economies of the two countries. A vicious system, euphemistically called "military balance," is the modern rendering of the old policy of divide and rule. Sections of the dominant elites on both sides of the border are willing partners in this quiet conspiracy. Deliberately under-played is the realization that such problems erode both stability and security in the long run.

Meanwhile, Britain, Australia, New Zealand, and now various island pockets in the Indian Ocean, are projected as providing a so-called invisible stabilizing external presence. There is deep reluctance to view their role through Asian eyes. These remnants of an empire should no longer be accepted by us as independent factors, only as junior partners of the USA. More relevant in the Asian context is the industrial muscle of Europe and how it can be used to break the parallelism of the major external power. Asia is beginning at last to seek more flexibility in her trade and commerce—and this is a significant pointer to the future.

The USA is paraded as the main bulwark against communist aggression—the Chinese variety or otherwise—but the dangerous polarizing effect of the physical US presence in Asia is minimized. This polarization places an unhealthy emphasis on expensive and politically explosive military establishments, wrecks genuine economic growth and creates frustrations which open the way for violent take-overs. The story of Viet Nam, as considered by us, is very different from the accounts popularized officially by the external powers. Indeed, we are deeply disturbed by the possibility of these cynical interventions increasing in Asia and Africa and embroiling our peoples in military escalations over which we have little or no control. Yet, so assertive is the continental presence of the external powers, that no coordinated moves have been made to highlight the dangers of this kind of "protection" and to evolve alternative, transitionary systems of security.

It is important to realize the transitionary nature of the immediate security psychosis. The carefully phased withdrawal of the external powers—through a skilful mix of compulsion and persuasion—would create in its wake a profound metamorphosis in Asia. It would nurture more viable concepts of co-existence within Asia and between Asia and the rest of the world at political, economic, military and social levels. China, isolated and angry, still posing the major questionmark in any debate on

Asian security, would be put under new disciplines, and we would strengthen those sections of Chinese opinion which oppose Maoist aberrations. Political, economic and military polarizations only feed her traditional ambitions by seriously disturbing stability in Asia.

If the nations of Asia are serious about the business of "protecting" themselves, they will have to establish a dialogue among themselves on all problems and to insulate these problems from incendiary external influences. There are no problems which cannot be tackled in rationality and in good faith. The external presence distorts the dialogue, often makes it a recognizable echo of the conflicting needs of the major powers. Too long have we accepted this depressing and frustrating state of affairs as inevitable.

Within the framework of such an assessment, India would have to design a policy which would safeguard her national interests and also strengthen Asian security and stability. So long as no spheres of influence are sought, it is possible for India to fuse her national interests with those of the region. A policy which reinforces Asian sovereignty in Asia has to be consciously sponsored at various levels—political, economic and military. The slurring over of this perspective in the course of the cold war, and the conflicts spawned by it, is one of the critical and central facts of the present situation.

The objectives of such a policy would be in terms of the following priorities.

(*a*) Full recognition to the nations of Asia in the United Nations as the first step towards evolving a mutually agreed Asian machinery for the solution of outstanding questions inherited largely from an imperialist-colonialist past.

(*b*) A disengagement plan to be implemented on critical Asian problems even as the external powers begin their withdrawal from the continent, including peripheral areas.

(*c*) Active encouragement to the formation on a federal basis of larger compact groupings of nations, particularly in those areas where the existence of partitioned or tiny helpless States attracts local and external intervention.

(*d*) The sponsorship of Asian institutions which cut across the present tension-enveloped divisions within the continent and which help foster the opinion for genuine co-existence and stability on the continent.

(*e*) Sponsorship of Asian collaboration in all fields, including science and technology.

Admittedly, the broad formulation of such a policy, and its breakdown into a plan of action, is immediately confronted by the misunderstandings and tensions inherited by and created in Asia during the first half of this century. We should be only too aware from the start of these challenges to rationality, for only then will we develop the courage and dynamism required to break the present acceptance of a damaging status quo based on the deliberate and cynical partitioning of countries, or panicky pressures to isolate this or that Asian trend on calculations which have no relevance to the genuine and long-term interests of Asia.

We cannot accept the subtle popularization of an Asian polarization on the plea that there is no other way to security. Positive and meaningful answers are not to be found in the lazy acceptance of present-day aberrations as the valid dimensions for future action, but in a vigorous effort to evolve a new frame within which a more durable balance of power can be achieved in Asia by the Asian nations. A total approach is demanded comparable to the total approach of the external powers.

I believe that the political mood which could create the sanctions for this approach exists in large measure, even though it needs careful focusing. The implications of a new strategic line in foreign policy thinking also need to be understood more thoroughly, for only then can appropriate tactics be designed to achieve the twin objectives of Asian security and stability. India's attitudes will condition developments and for this reason it is vital that her present vulnerable economic and political condition should not be exploited to paralyze her initiatives for an Asian solution to Asia's problems.

Our foreign policy and defence planners tend to take divergent paths. The political and economic cost of this exercise is crippling. A fusion of thought is demanded and it will have to base itself on three inter-locked concepts which are beginning to crystallize.

(*a*) That the policy of non-alignment will undergo transformations to the extent that Asian motivations and aspirations dictate.

(*b*) That the nations of Asia will increasingly formulate their basic policies on realistic adjustments within Asia, particularly as they tend towards economic independence.

(*c*) That the attitude of the nations of Asia to the external powers will be moulded by the common interests of the continent.

Such conclusions may appear idealistic and startling in the context of the assumptions normally made about Asia. But why should Asia develop responses different from those formulated in Europe, North America or Latin America. This approach may be criticized as largely economistic, but we must ask ourselves why it should be otherwise when the mechanics of markets and economic growth are beginning to impact policy more profoundly than concepts of military power. We must take note of these qualitative changes in our world system or continue as manipulatable pawns in the power game of super powers, pseudo super powers and their junior partners. The choice in the final analysis is ours.

21

Politics of Power*

Who are the major powers?

There are two super powers—the USA and the USSR—so described because they command massive nuclear capability. They have global interests, too, and one interest impinges on the other. They are also forever concerned as to how policies should unfold in various regions, without even the threat of destruction to themselves.

In Asia, from an Indian subcontinental point of view, there are two major powers in addition to the super powers who have direct interest in our region: Japan, packing the power of an industrial giant, and China beginning to assert herself as a result of her impressive self-reliant capacities in the interrelated economic, political and military fields. Japan and China must of necessity be interested in the Indian subcontinent, which exerts influence throughout South and South-East Asia, and in the strategic Indian ocean.

I would also like to throw into our calculations the presence of another kind of force which in the context of general underdevelopment is likely increasingly to impact events on the Indian subcontinent. I refer to the ideological force. In our setting it is not just communist. It can be Islamic. Both these ideologies are rigid, fervent doctrines which command an allegiance spilling over frontiers and blurring them. Within the struggle of the

*From *Seminar*, 146; October 1971.

super and major powers, this ideological force is exploited openly or subtly, and we cannot ignore it.

Now, what is the Indian subcontinent? It is obviously the area
covered by India and Pakistan. This is only too clear. But if we
are to comprehend the Indian subcontinent's involvements with
the major external powers and the problems of Indian security,
we cannot do this in isolation from what goes on in Afghanistan,
Iran, Ceylon, Burma, the Andamans and Nicobars, the Maldives,
Madagascar, the Seychelles and the Himalayan kingdom. These
territories on the periphery of the Indian subcontinent should
be of vital concern to us, for developments in any of these areas
have an immediate bearing on the Indian subcontinent.

And, finally, what do we mean by security? Security from
what, for what? In the course of any argumentation on security
we could come to the conclusion that we seek security for our
sovereignty, for our sovereign will. Security which sacrifices
sovereignty is not security but something else.

Having touched upon the definitions, let us proceed to take a
look at the power (political and security) situation in this region. May be, we can develop a perspective for the seventies.

In September 1971, there can be no starting point other than
the Indo-Soviet Treaty just concluded. It marks, despite state-
ments to the contrary, a major turning point in our external
relations. But before we analyze this treaty, we must dwell somewhat on what might be called "the surrounding situation," the
backdrop to the treaty.

The war in Viet Nam, which has conditioned so much of our
thinking in international developments, is now in a state of
stalemate. The stalemate marks the defeat of the US military
machine and is bound to release many repercussions within the
US system. To salvage some kind of credibility, the US State
Department has been compelled to undertake a wide ranging
review of its various "scenarios"—strategic and tactical exercises
designed to cope with "situations."

What is now emerging is an attempt to refocus on the Soviet
Union as the main competitor—and enemy—to the USA.
The Kissinger visit to Peking, the projected Nixon visit to China
"in sack-cloth and ashes," so to say, the "devaluation" of the
dollar, the emergency measures being taken to correct the imbalances developing internally in the USA, all these are part of

an effort to consolidate the military-industrial complex in the USA against the USSR during a very complex period of transition. The "style" is impressive, but we must remember the many objectives, including the US presidential election towards the end of 1972.

The Soviet Union has every reason to be disturbed by the trends which have been set in motion. For some years now, the leadership in Moscow has been worried by the increasingly heavy burden of defence spending and military commitments abroad. This confrontation with the USA is unequal in the sense that the Soviet people have to sacrifice much more for military purposes than the American people. Moscow knows that the burden cannot continue unequal.

Then, again, adventures abroad, as in the Arab world, have misfired. The Soviet Union, despite the aid given, has met the fate of all aid-givers. It has been isolated, and since President Nasser's death a new nationalism seems to be stirring in West Asia. Now the US gambit to strike a deal with a China that does not trust Soviet intentions must cause grave misgivings in Moscow because it makes sensitive the USSR's sprawling border with China the longest border in the world.

India is a naturally seen as a countervailing force against China to be strengthened and consolidated in South and South-East Asia. But the old, discredited techniques prevail—pacts and treaties which have the effect of destroying what they set out to achieve. The "ugly American," the "hated Yankee" can become the "ugly Russian" and the "hated Ruski." We have recent examples.

In other words, the super powers, whether of capitalistic or communistic persuasion, have not been able to build spheres of friendship and understanding. Tiny elites may serve their purposes, but the broad movements of people are mercurial, and extremely sensitive to being reduced to anything which approximates to a junior partner status.

China understands this fully, having extricated herself from "a pact of friendship" with the USSR. Peking designs her internal and external policies as a growing power anxious to become the leader of all those who have been disillusioned in the embrace of the super powers. Each nuance of policy seeks to emphasize that only those nations are friends of China who refuse to play second fiddle to the super powers—yes, even a country like "revisionist," socialist, Yugoslavia which has departed from the orthodox doctrines of communist practice.

Of course, nuclear China is feared. Traditionally, her attempt to pose as the only major force in Asia suggests a chauvinism which can become extremely dangerous for neighbours, big and small. For India, the experience of the past decade is a warning. Even at the best of times, India's continental unity is treated with reserve by Peking. In other words, single-nation China has little understanding of the multinational coherence of the Indian subcontinent.

Broadly, we can assume that the motivations of the super powers and the intendent super power will remain more or less constant in the course of the surface transformations that international relations will undergo in the course of the present decade. Only an unforeseen catastrophe or a drastic change in the balance of power could alter these broad motivations. It is not my intention to speculate on the unforeseen. I can only take the trends as they are developing and study their inherent logic on the situation in the India subcontinent. I have already defined this area as something more than the land encompassed by the boundaries of the Indian Republic.

A major and profound development has taken place on the Indian subcontinent. The people of East Pakistan, in rebellion against the colonial regime of Islamabad in West Pakistan, have moved beyond the politics of the partition era. The rebellion was legitimatized by an extraordinary election which gave the Awami League a fantastic near-unanimous vote. The secular character of the movement in East Pakistan struck at the roots of the partition policies of British imperialism and provided the first faint outlines of a possible communal understanding on the subcontinent proper. The emotions released have to find satisfaction in a settlement which will see the establishment of a sovereign Bangladesh. The actions now being taken will determine what kind of future the subcontinent will create for itself.

It is interesting that the initiatives of Moscow, Washington and Peking were in the directions of freezing the situation as it were. India responded, feeling friendless, fearful and fuzzy about objectives. Only the fortunate coincidence of the Pakistani hijacking of an Indian plane, which gave Delhi the justification to

ban Pakistan's overflights to Dacca and to complicate the rein-
forcing of army establishments in East Bengal, was exploited.
Otherwise, we marked time, even though the situation in the
East was weighted in our favour. We rationalized by saying that
world reaction would be against us if we intervened. Specialists
all over the world were amazed at our "restraint"—the same
"restraint" which was praised by governments interested in the
status quo.

In the second phase, millions began moving on to our frontiers
seeking refuge from the brutalities of the genocide. Again, our
lack of preparations and calculations is seized upon by the
dominant powers to blunt our frontiers to the refugees as this
would have meant shooting down those who attempted to
cross. No government could survive such an act. So the search
began for alternatives. Attention turned to the Mukti Fouj.
Immediately, inspired propaganda warned of the possibility that
the Fouj would fall into Maoist control.

As the suppression of the military junta proceeded, vital weeks
were lost speculating on the political repercussions of assisting
the freedom fight in Bangladesh. The demand for recognition of
the Bangladesh Government—designed to push the GOI into
action—was described as adventurist in the context of what the
GOI was planning. It was made known, to assuage public
opinion, that guerilla activity by the Mukti Fouj would intensify
and keep the Pakistani militarists occupied until such time as the
neutralization of the Chinese Himalayan threat could be achieved. Then military action by India would take place in order to
end the military terror in Bangladesh and make possible the
return of some five million refugees. The stepping up of guerilla
activity by the Bangladesh authorities implied, inevitably, the
lifting of political control over the Mukti Fouj. All those who
wanted to take up arms were given the chance to do so. By now,
the world was responding to the trauma of Bangladesh.

The staggering size of the refugee problem and the threat of
epidemics did what no propaganda could. A wave of repulsion
against Pakistani atrocities offered the promise of relief for the
refugees. To numb Indian responses, the impression sponsored
was that international action would discipline Pakistan and the
refugees would return. India was naturally urged to continue her
remarkable restraint in the handling of the situation.

In the third phase, the military junta in Pakistan was able to claim a certain degree of consolidation. President Yahya began to threaten India with dire consequences. More revelations were made about the supply of arms to Pakistan through various sources, including the USA. The USSR resorted to equidistant reportage between the versions supplied by India and Pakistan. China's aid to Pakistan was highlighted. Despite a good international press, India was made to feel isolated. The UN stepped in with the proposal for observers on the border to inhibit Indian action. At this moment, the Kissinger visit was announced. He was reported to be anxious for an on-the-spot investigation of the situation. We know what the visit was about, but there was a significant follow-up. On his return to the USA, Kissinger summoned our Ambassador and provided him with some "research"—that the Chinese would not be passive spectators in an Indo-Pakistani conflict, and the USA would not be able to help India in any way—research already peddled through other parties in India. In other words, India had better watch out. A full circle as it were.

In the fourth phase, the thesis was now orchestrated in various supposedly knowledgeable circles, within India and outside, that the Pakistani military junta might risk war rather than permit India to aid Bangladesh, that China would be an active ally should Pakistan decide to act. The thesis found a ready response in critical policy-making areas in India. The next act of the drama was ordered. An "Indian Kissinger" took off for Moscow and brought back a twenty-year treaty of friendship and cooperation. It was signed with extraordinary speed.

Twenty-five years of non-alignment were written off overnight. Nevertheless, we are assured that the treaty strengthens non-alignment. Significantly, the treaty is welcomed both in the USSR and the USA. China doesn't comment. Bangladesh is the first issue to be tackled. It is made clear twenty-four hours later in a joint communique on East Pakistan—no longer Bangladesh! —that a political solution is to be sought in the interests of "all the people of Pakistan." The war fever recedes. The stock markets recover. There is extraordinary relief throughout India. We are not alone. We have a friend—a super power.

We are in the fifth phase now. We are convincing ourselves that the refugees will have to stay. After all, never in history have refugees returned to the scene of genocide. We are assuring ourselves that no more refugees will cross the border, even though famine threatens. Reports are circulating about how the Mujib trial might yield a solution to the tangles in Pakistan, that the USSR may seek another level of Tashkent diplomacy. At the same time, guerilla experts are educating us not to expect in the immediate future any great developments from the Mukti Fouj, now named Mukti Bahani.

China watches these developments in silence. The liberation struggle in Bangladesh is passing into new hands, young activists who are risking their lives daily along the waterways of Sonar Bangla. The original nationalist leadership of the Awami League need not remain at the helm. And so, if Pakistan is a US base and India a Soviet ally, why can't Bangladesh look to Peking. The thought begins to find adherents. It is part of the realpolitik of the region.

The phases in the response on Bangladesh are a significant pointer to the interests and policies of the major powers in the Indian subcontinent and the specific problem of Indian security. Let me pinpoint them. Then we will know where there is convergence and where there is conflict. The Soviet Union's view has the following major dimensions:

1. The partition of the subcontinent was unfortunate. It prevented the growth of an Asian power capable of balancing the influence of China.

2. The Indian federal policy is viable. It must be strengthened in such a way as to diffuse fissiparous tendencies.

3. India must be equipped to become militarily a countervailing force against China. The border problems have made this possible.

4. India should be more active in projecting a sphere of influence in South and South-East Asia. She should not leave China unchallenged. Such neglect would endanger her future. Hence the need for a Soviet-sponsored Asian Collective Security Pact.

5. The consolidation of the region behind the Soviet Union is closely bound up with the emerging Soviet presence in the Indian Ocean. This presence, in the long run, will require military bases and facilities in South and South-East Asia, as

also along the African coast. The ideological thrust should be
underplayed to assist these ends.

6. West Pakistan is important, as is Afghanistan, for through
these territories the Soviet Union could build an easy land
access to the countries of the Indian Ocean—that is, after a
consolidated presence is established in the Indian Ocean—and
into the Oceanic islands of the area.

7. East Bengal must be insulated against the pressures of the
Maoists—or else Peking will also enter the Indian Ocean.

The Soviet Union is groping for the formulation of a coherent
short-term and long-term policy. The policy-makers in Moscow
are "activists" at a time when the leadership of the USA is lick-
ing its wounds.

The USA's view of the subcontinent is different in many respects, even though super power collusion exists at various levels:

1. The partition of the subcontinent marked an acceptance
of the reality of Hindu-Muslim animosity. Pakistan is a trust-
ed friend and has genuine fears about Indian revanchism. But
India's friendship is not to be discarded. She needs economic
assistance and such assistance creates some stability in the
area.

2. The strange structure of Pakistan calls for sensitive state-
craft. An independent East Bengal would only become a
colony of India. A confederal set-up is possibly the best solution for Pakistan.

3. Pakistan is an excellent base for the USA. Her leadership, military and civilian, is practical and coherent unlike the
complex Indian elite. The military balance between India and
Pakistan has to be relative, but visible. War between them is
to be prevented. In this sense, the Chinese presence in the
Himalayas is not to be dismissed. It cautions India.

4. Pakistan cannot play a major role in the region, but in
the context of Islamic power politics it asserts a major influence in an arc extending from Morocco to Indonesia. India is
a gap, but even in the gap there are 60 million Muslims. In
other words, Pakistan cannot be abandoned in the interest of
short-term gains.

5. The future of this region is largely dependent on the

progress of understanding between the USA and China. In the international balance of power, such an understanding would tremendously weaken the Soviet Union's influence in the region. Again, Pakistan's friendly links with China, and the solution of their border problems makes Islamabad a factor in the future.

6. Admittedly, the pattern of economic growth, built upon military spending, militates against the Bengal sector, but there is no reason why more should not be done to improve the lot of the Bengalis. This has been a major lapse.

7. East Bengal must be isolated from the pressures of Maoists. Not only must Peking be kept out of this area, but troubles in East Pakistan would spark a break up of West Pakistan's Punjabis, Pathans, Baluchis, and Sindhis. These animosities are a common threat to India and Pakistan. This should be driven home.

In other words, the USA's approach to policy-making in the region is very much more established, clear-cut and, one might say, consistent. National interests are pursued, but there is a greater amount of resource to create the impression of impartiality and generosity.

China's view is more difficult to decipher, but let me try and summarize a probable one.

1. The partition of the subcontinent was the first inevitable step in the break up of an artificial entity. The subcontinent will break up into its national groups. Only China is a major nation in Asia.

2. Everything must be done to encourage the break up of the subcontinent, but not openly.

3. India can never be a serious countervailing force against China. She can play this role only in alliance with the USSR or the USA. Such alliances should spark anger within India, but these reactions may be blunted by hostility over the border troubles with China. India must, therefore, be skilfully devalued in the eyes of Asians to reduce her usefulness to the USA and the USSR.

4. There is likely to be serious conflict between Chinese and Indian interests in South-East Asia, but the skills of the over-

seas Chinese community should be able to neutralize the Indians politically and commercially. A more active role in East Africa and the islands of the Indian Ocean (particularly Ceylon) is stressed.

5. China's prestige builds because of its successes at home and because of its sovereign presence abroad. This must be maintained now with advanced US technological collaboration. Interference in the internal affairs of other nations must be denounced in public—even if in private it is encouraged. Confidence in China as a friend must be built. South and South-East Asia's suspicions must be dissolved.

6. Friendship with India is difficult, but Pakistan, seeking psychological support in alliances with big powers, is a natural ally in the struggle against Indian intrigues. Verbal military support is enough. A threat is enough. The Indian after 1962 is easily impacted.

7. Nothing must be done to give the impression that China wishes a Maoist Bangladesh. This development will take place as a result of the logic of the liberation movement which will increasingly pass from the nationalist to revolutionary cadre. China will then have a base on the vital subcontinent. This will mark the beginning of the break-up of the subcontinent.

China's view is essentially that of an ideologically motivated single-nation State obsessed by its desire to lead Asia. The only possible threat to this desire could come from India in South Asia. Japan is too small in today's context to matter.

At this point, it is necessary to take note of the views of a number of nations which, together, pack a mighty punch—even though, individually, they can be dismissed as inconsequential in the politics of the region. I think it would be short-sighted to imagine that these nations will continue to tread their lonely paths. Increasingly, as the giants converge on the spoils of their power game, and China joins in these smaller nations might well act for a more collective and sovereign assertion. India can very well be a catalyst in this development if she is not inhibited by the new Indo-Soviet treaty.

Let me run over some of the possibilities.

1. Japan, following the US financial squeeze against her

export trade, and viewing with some alarm the Sino-US detente, cannot possibly carry on as before. New alignments with massive commercial ramifications will be sought, preferably with regions still free of super power involvement. Even the USSR and China are probing possibilities with Japan. But India remains aloof.

2. In South-East Asia, Indonesia and the Phillippines are ready for independent thinking and action. But India remains distant.

3. East Africa moves in the same direction, though with greater suspicions of the motives of others. But India does not move.

4. The European Community must be wondering too about its future in Asia, particularly industrial nations like France, and Germany. But India is content to act the spectator.

5. Australia and Canada also cannot be lumped together with the UK or the USA in discussions on Asia. But India does not enter into a dialogue.

The position which is developing suggests that whereas the super powers and the aspiring super powers are moving to demarcate areas of influence and control in our part of the world, new options are opening for India at this critical time. Unfortunately, the hastily organized Indo-Soviet Treaty has put a brake on these developments, but if we are to build a security system which is sovereign and not at the mercy of super power calculations we will have to do some total thinking on our internal economic consolidation and our independent external presence. We must, in other words, seek to become another centre of power. I shall try to fix some of the priorities and leave the rest to you.

1. Bangladesh cannot be allowed to fester. The refugee waves can destroy political stability in India. If we remain passive spectators, it may become necessary to insulate east India to prevent the collapse of the rest of the economy. A sovereign Bangladesh, established as speedily as possible, is now a vital national task. The joint communique with the Soviet Union suggests otherwise. A slow liberation movement will not solve our refugee problem and will open the way to

deeper external intrigues on our subcontinent.

2. With the signing of the Indo-Soviet Treaty, we have entered the power game. Our immediate need is to fill the gaps in our collaborative economy to give us some degree of self reliance. These gaps must be filled by the Soviet Union, much in the same way as a balanced industrial base was provided for China. We cannot allow ourselves to remain at the mercy of aid-givers and suppliers. A compact of friendship must create the basis for equality.

3. In the context of equality, an immediate decision is needed to embark on a nuclear armament programme. Its scale and depth are complex problems, but we can no longer remain outside the nuclear game. We would then condemn ourselves to junior partnership—and lose our "presence" in the Indian Ocean. What's more we must establish this presence most firmly and with skill. The recent Ceylon eruption was a warning.

4. We must search out alliances with non-super powers, but powers who possess industrial capacity and strategic facilities. A series of alliances could again open the options closed by the Indo-Soviet Treaty. And we should not neglect the possibility of an equation with China. It may provide a key to our new power role.

5. At home, an austere mass line to mobilize resources, to strengthen national morale, to break defeatism, demoralization and cynical apathy will have to be sketched. The mass line is very different from the euphoric socialism sponsored by the ruling party. It is in the nature of a democratic cultural revolution comparable to the happenings in China and because it is democratic and in a federal set up, it is extremely difficult to carry through.

This should be the new perspective before us. To work it out would require immense intellectual effort, physical planning and dedicated implementation. Many pressure groups, sponsored by interested powers, will seek to confuse and blunt such an effort. They must be defeated by sovereign men and women.

22

Our Security Scenario*

The critical fact that Pakistan is today half the State it was, must inevitably mould political and diplomatic thinking within the region and outside. Much of the debate which takes place today about the Pakistani capacity to mount new threats, in collusion with China or the USA, fails to take this fact into full consideration. We tend to be obsessed by the security dimensions of the past. This mood will pass, hopefully, and then India will begin to appreciate the qualitative change which has occurred in South Asia.

A rapid summary of the international scene will bear out this qualitative change in the background against which our security system has to be planned.

A major development is the sustained effort of President Nixon to arrange a detente with Chairman Mao. Increasingly, this aspect of US foreign policy influences all other initiatives emanating from Washington. How far China will go to accommodate the USA remains to be seen, but if her present psychopathic fear of Soviet power is any indication, the honeymoon should be of considerable duration. China obviously views the Pakistani debacle in Bangladesh as a significant setback to her interests, for the new-found credibility of India, as seen from Peking, strengthens a Soviet backed countervailing force against China in South Asia. After all, the Tibetan border is 6000 miles

*From *Seminar*, 150; February 1972.

from Peking and the Indian Army is not the bedraggled division-and-a-half of 1962. The Chinese are realists and know that no easy victories, cease-fire and withdrawals are possible in the seventies.

The USA, or at least that portion of it which thinks within the equation of Nixon and Kissinger, revealed its perspectives in the course of the recent liberation of Bangladesh. Pakistan is seen as the only base in South Asia to challenge the new Soviet presence in the Indian Ocean. Economically, it is very viable. Politically, it will settle down. Given time, it could become the anchor of the Islamic world in South Asia. In other words, the further break up of Pakistan is not inevitable.

A quite different view emerges from Moscow. The USSR is now at least interested in Indian credibility in South Asia. With the USA and China moving into a detente situation, the countries in South and South-East Asia, view the future with a certain measure of apprehension. The Soviet Union would like to see India play a prominent anti-US role in the region, which would be indirectly aimed at Chinese influence. The recent change in the attitude of India to Hanoi is an interesting pointer. Indian credibility, diplomatic and military, is a source of strength to the USSR in its complex dealing with Maoism. In other words, unlike the involvement in the Arab world, Moscow-India relations provide a two-way system of cooperation and collaboration. This is a healthy backdrop for the Indo-Soviet Treaty and can help neutralize the natural propensity of a super power to exploit its relationship with a weaker partner.

For the first time, the European Community and Japan watch the changes taking place with a strong desire to re-open their options on several issues. In many ways, these industrially powerful regions are of vital concern to the manipulations of the super powers. The carefully worked out plans and scenarios under scrutiny in various leading capitals can be thrown into confusion by unexpected postures on the part of Europe and Japan. Both seek freedom of manoeuvre and refuse to be taken for granted. Both can swing the odds against this or that super power and its allies. Both will be wooed. And both will take decisions on the basis of hard practical advantage. Any analysis of international alignments today must take into account which of the two super power systems offers the possibilities of equal trade and mutually beneficial development. It is no longer a situation where the confrontation is between ideologically opposed blocs there is a mixture of ideologies in both blocs and in the uncommitted areas. All this makes for the assertion of national interests or regional interests.

This is the canvas against which India will plan her security in the seventies. Again, Pakistan and China will provide the key to the planning. Let us look at the situation as it now unfolds.

Pakistan, half its size, cannot hope to build any military threat against India without massive external assistance. Loose talk about another Israel only serves to illustrate the total lack of information on the internal roots of the Israeli posture against the flabby Arabs and the kind of military support provided to that posture by external agencies. To become a gendarme of either the USA or China, Pakistan would once again risk its internal coherence. Military power would inevitably concentrate in the heartlands of the Punjab and spark old, internal hostilities among the Pathans and the Baluchis. Bangladesh is a dramatic precedent, capable of emulation. In pursuing the path of revanchism against India, Pakistan would be embarked on a self-destroying mission.

China is in a position somewhat different to Pakistan but, in military terms, rather hedged in. Her vast border with the Soviet Union demands the permanent deployment of millions of men. And, now, India, in the South can no longer be bullied. Estimates put the present strength of the Indian Army in the Himalayas at 10 mountain divisions, highly trained and equipped with the latest destructive power. To speak from a position of strength, China would have to nearly double her existing garrison of some 13 divisions in Tibet and keep them serviced at the end of a rather frail 6000 mile supply line. A military miscalculation by China would damage her prestige quite severely throughout the world. Peking would rather trade on her so-called victory of 1962.

Of course, the protagonists for a nuclear programme will argue that all these calculations change the moment China possesses the capacity to obliterate a major city in either the USA or the USSR. Then, it is argued, China can blackmail her underdeveloped neighbours, knowing that the super powers will not risk their cities for some far off, expendable communities. These calculations overlook a host of other factors which persuade nations to enter wars even though not directly threatened. That is how local wars become world wars. And it would also be naive to imagine that nuclear capacities will remain confined to a few nations during the decade we are entered upon.

The Indo-Soviet Treaty of Friendship, originally proposed by the USSR two years ago when its border troubles were escalating with China and Maoism was beginning a detente with its traditional enemies and flexing its muscles for confrontations within the communist system, was finally pushed by the Indian leadership. This was at the end of 1971 when it appeared as if Pakistan was to be given a US and China-backed leverage to pressurize and paralyze the subcontinent into accepting a shattering refugee burden. The compact as such was merely a confirmation of the natural friendship between India and the Soviet Union whose interests did not conflict, but the very logic of the compact brought India into the game of power. From now on it would be necessary to seek out spheres of influence, to outflank and corner potential adversaries, and to build the kind of political and diplomatic thrust which tastes of major power status.

The political and military developments over Bangladesh have speedily crystallized a new balance of power and heightened India's relevance in South Asia. Delhi's decision, for example, suddenly to recognize the Democratic Republic of Viet Nam in Hanoi marks the start of a new and active phase in regional diplomacy. It may appear on the surface to be a slap in the face of the USA now busy again bombing North Viet Nam after delivering homilies on peace to the GOI. The more perceptive will see it as an action designed to contrast sharply with the opportunist silence of Peking. Hanoi has responded more than warmly, and it would not be out of context to expect many such initiatives in the reigon.

There is nothing Kautilyan about these developments. We are now compact-bound to support causes which are mutually beneficial to the interests of both the USSR and India. It is equally clear that despite all previous attempts to keep our options open, Indo-Soviet diplomacy will demarcate Chinese threats, singly or in alliance, and neutralize them in such a way that Peking stands exposed as an unprincipled operator, and

not as the charismatic ideological force that it seeks to appear
to be. Many interesting scenarios can emerge from this diplomatic play.

In Europe, and in Japan, we are today witnessing an extraordinary euphoria about China and the pristine quality of Maoism.
The mass media, irrespective of ownership and control, are in
many ways feeding this euphoria which reflects in passing the
almost naive US discovery of communist China. The fear of
Russia, the anger against those who, like India, side with the
Kremlin, the satisfaction over China's successful attempts to
crack and splinter the rigid, hierarchical, international communist movement, and the developing detente between the USA
and China which will, it is hoped, isolate the Soviet Union,
provide the motives behind current diplomatic thinking. In other
words, China is seen as the giant that will change the balance
of world power. But will it? A series of trends are developing
which refuse to be subverted to serve these ends.

These trends are based on the economic realities prevailing
in the world. If Europe as a continent sees itself capable of
striking an independent path in economic relations with the rest
of the international community, and particularly the developing
world which is suspicious of US aid, how much more susceptible
is Japan to pulls which would detach it from the pressures of
Washington. The hard-headed industrial managers in Japan, who
live by importing raw materials and exporting finished goods at
highly competitive prices, cannot but be attracted by the opportunity to exploit the riches of Siberia and to market both capital
and consumer goods through the sprawling spaces of an increasingly prosperous USSR. Underdeveloped China offers no such
prospects for at least another twenty or thirty years, for she is
concerned only with acquiring vital higher technology from the
USA during an uncertain detente.

The euphoria about China cannot last. When everyone boun-
ces back to reality, a very much more complex system of power
balance will prevail in each region of the world. The rigid
models of communist and capitalist orthodoxy are no longer
relevant. The new models have not been formulated. Until they
are, we will seem to be drifting into all manner of confused and
contradictory positions but only for a while, for after Nixon

and Mao have had their first parleys, the descent to reality will begin.

In this situation, India is in a critical position. Her effectiveness, both as interventionist in international politics and as a sovereign power capable of defending herself, will depend largely on the skill with which the internal situation is handled at the political level and at the economic. For 25 years we have lived on the belief that our country is large enough to ensure that friendly aid and assistance can be received from all and sundry. Some of these day dreams have been shattered. But we have still to gear ourselves to an independent power role—yes, independent even, if need be, of our present friends. When we begin to act on this consciousness, the full dimensions of the challenge will take shape.

23

Foreign Policy*

It would not be unfair to state that India's foreign policy over recent years has survived brutal exposure only because of the general confusion prevailing in international relations following the collapse of the old power policies which were based on rigid spheres of influence and marginal manipulative areas. Today, the manipulatable area has increased dramatically. The former spheres of influence, except at the inner core, are pushing for some kind of sovereign existence. The change is major, qualitative, but there is no reflection of this change in Delhi's current thinking on foreign affairs.

The extraordinary sustained initiative to arrange a much belated detente on the subcontinent, following the rise of Bangladesh should not be seen as a reorientation of foreign policy even though it is projected as such. The detentist policy is dictated by the need to concentrate resources on internal changes and to abandon policies which appear to the world as designed to spark large scale communal riots in the subcontinent. Whether in India, Pakistan or Bangladesh, the essential striving will have to be for a meaningful peace and solid collaboration. In this context, the developing detente on the subcontinent, despite the hysterical punctuation marks from Rawalpindi (or Islamabad!), is unlikely to influence, as some believe, the unfolding of India's foreign policy. The Pakistan thorn is no longer a viable weapon of embarrassment. And international diplomacy is now in no

*From *Seminar*, 186; February 1975.

doubt about the role that India willy nilly has to play in South Asia. I say this quite conscious of the internal strains wracking the subcontinent. A dispassionate viewing of the situation in South Asia offers several significant pointers and questions to the future.

1. The massive U.S. intervention in Vietnam, made impotent by the resistance of the ordinary people of North and South Vietnam, has ended and old type polarizations are dissolving.

2. As a result of the partial withdrawal of the military presences of the super powers, the region is at last beginning to look inwards, at itself, and to assess the potentialities of fuller cooperation between the countries of the area.

3. The new sovereign mood, despite the pitfalls of the current international economic situation, feeds angry protests against any discriminatory or predatory economic presence, such as that of Japan in recent years.

4. The old political equations are under pressure. The Generals collapse in Thailand before a youthful democratic upsurge, the Generals attempt at consolidation in Indonesia after the uncertainties of the Sukarno era, and in Burma the Generals begin to open up the country.

5. The Indian Ocean attracts the attention of the powerful navies of the world. A vacuum is to be filled and the hunt for bases is open and energetic, particularly from the western nations who have no reliable allies.

6. The battle over oil and its price has educated the policy planners of the region about the real base of western affluence and the need once again to fight determinedly for fair prices for the raw materials of South Asia.

7. Naturally, attention is concentrated on those nations in the region and in West Asia who command the oil-fields. Here is new wealth to transform backwardness, but will it be so used?

8. Iran in South Asia, and Saudi Arabia, are the two pillars of the new oil rich and much of the diplomatic manoeuvres of the nations of South Asia will be between the two.

9. Islamic summitry intensifies as the millions from oil sales are ammassed. Will this summitry develop secular pos-

tures or will we witness the worst faction fights between the "brotherhood" of Islamic States?

10. Will the detente between the super powers reduce the options for the nations of the region or open a more positive climate of peace for populations whose economic conditions are about the most depressed in the world?

It is only natural that India's foreign policy must root itself first in these new realities of the region before elaborating its attitudes further afield. Our relationship with the Soviet Union despite its close involvement with the region, cannot ignore the competitive and pervasive power of the USA, with its known surpluses and advanced technologies, and the growing power identities of the European Community and Japan. And China, hostile for various geo-political reasons, creates reactions and counter-reactions which influence attitudes towards the Indian subcontinent, for example, Sikkim, Nepal and Bhutan.

It would not be an exaggeration to say that the state has now arrived in international relations where societies which have inflated their standards of living and are preparing (marginally!) to shed fat are frightened by the prospect of tackling the poverty of the Indian subcontinent out of their own resources. The honeymoon is over. The affluent are tremendously motivated by the achievements of Maoist China, austere, egalitarian, self-reliant. They would that other developing peoples were equally so, particularly the over-populated land mass of the subcontinent of India. And they are not bothered about the "methods," so long as these do not encroach upon their systems.

In other words, the fact that Indian democracy fails to tackle the problems of poverty is just too bad. If communism scores then the browns and blacks had better learn the lesson. The old missionary zeal about getting the job done "in freedom" has dissolved in the face of the creeping economic crisis which closes in on the affluent pockets of the world. Yes, this view is too conditioned by the impulses of the moment, but then, who is there to care. We are now told: affluence is a wasteful business, and its going to take time to discipline it. Don't follow us. Live in civilized simplicity. We will love you all the more.

There is nothing superficial about how such a standpoint influences international relations. The dedicated cadres of Com-

munist China are a model. The lazy, grasping, imitative elites
of the developing world are no longer sought. They are the
cancer. Apply this psychology to India, and you begin to see
what is happening to the image of the subcontinent. The libe-
rals, the do-gooders, are now increasingly swelling the ranks of
the China lobby in the west. The reactionaries who cannot
stomach anything to do with the socialist world, are compelled
to speak for the corrupt, democratic, developing world.

A foreign policy, essentially regional, and receiving a certain
recognition because of its closeness to a super power or power,
is possible to formulate in purely power political terms. For
example, India is big, a friend of the Soviet Union, commands a
fairly substantial military punch, is capable of retaliating
against neighbours without fundamental damage to the status
quo and cannot be subverted by the usual pressures. India is
playing some such regional role at present.

The moment we begin to speak of global postures, the limited
regional policy, dressed up in a lot of finery including an atomic
device, is exposed for the limited and blunt instrument that it is.
The theorists are deeply disturbed by the lack of global ambi-
tion, the noticeable silence on many critical international issues,
the lack of involvement in the common causes of the developing
world and the cynical use of "opportunities" in international
organizations. The elite in India imagines that these manifestations stem from a lazy and incompetent foreign service. This is
true, but only partially. The malaise is more serious.

To use the old cliche, the Indian has to put his house in order
before he can begin to speak on international issues. A leadership which over twenty-five years of freedom has failed to ensure drinking water for its people cannot talk in the style of a
major power. To emote about self-reliance, to build up a whole
super structure of controls to ensure sovereign decision-making,
to speak in the language of egalitarianism, and then to go begging for aid every year (even from the tiniest principalities of
the world!) is to ask for ridicule.

For India, this kind of challenge is terribly complex. Over
the past twenty-five years we have largely cut ourselves off from
the various currents of international and multi-national operation. We are, in other words, unsure of ourselves in a competitive world. We tend to bury ourselves in the complexities of our

subcontinent imagining that this is almost a total world, even though heavily aided and subsidized by the developed nations. The result: even when we have taken regional initiatives, as on the question of the Indian Ocean and on project collaboration with Iran and other Arab States, we are slow moving, uncertain, and basically fearful of stepping into the wider world. No amount of glib talk can hide this crisis of skills and psychology.

In facing the new realities, both global and regional, to which reference has been made earlier, the systems underpinning foreign policy formulation have to be drastically altered. The Foreign Office and its permanent service are quite incapable of understanding the role expected of them. Apart from the lack of specialized expertise, so necessary in these days of intense competition by professionally oriented personnel, significantly our foreign service is least interested in its own region, being motivated very largely in the direction of Europe and America.

In other words, the central instrument of our foreign policy, the foreign service, has to be reformed without delay. Certain guiding principles need to be observed.

1. All senior posts, both at home and abroad, must become highly selective, and not a matter of mechanical promotion.

2. Within the foreign service, average cadre must find its ceiling around the age of 48 and be blocked from further promotion. Special boards must be constituted to do the weeding.

3. Lateral entry must be ensured at every level of specialization—again through specifically constituted boards.

4. Intensive refresher training for all categories of the foreign service must be established to prevent the decay of capability, discipline and elan. This would mean involvement with national institutes.

5. The entire ministerial establishment calls for reorganization and modernization. The simplest mechanism of research briefing and feed-back are notable for their neglect by all and sundry.

6. A closer coordination between the leading echelons of the foreign service and the intelligence arm of the government has to be achieved despite inter-ministerial rivalries.

7. In the process of restructuring, the status of the Foreign Minister must be lifted to something more than a deputy to the Prime Minister, someone who merely carries the burden of another's policy.

Given a reorganization of the Foreign Office and its professional service, entered laterally with all the expertise we have in international politics and economics, there is no reason why a crisis-engulfed India cannot begin to take initiatives which are in her national interest, regionally and globally.

1. The careful mobilization of the talent, resource and cooperation of West, South and South-East Asia has yet to be launched despite all the sentiment in its favour. We have no concept of the region at the moment, or of the opportunities opening as a result of the new pricing of basic raw materials.

2. The reforging of non-aligned links on the basis of a hard-headed plan of cooperation between the developed and developing world does not seem to crystallize. It is a difficult but challenging task which must be faced sooner rather than later if we are to defuse the new tensions building between rich and poor nations.

3. The preparation of blueprints for the transformation of existing international agencies, including the UN family, into meaningful instruments has been too long delayed. This transformation is vital for the era now opening and which rejects these overpaid bureaucracies living on well-worn cliches and peripheral theorizing.

4. The careful formulation of collective initiatives immediately to redress the glaring inequalities and obvious malpractises embodied in the present day global system—a remarkably grey area which is now sought to be investigated by the newly sensitized conscience of mankind—demands the highest degree of political skill and commitment.

5. The extension of the struggle for peace and a drastic curtailment of expenditure on arms and armies has to be worked upon if the resources are to be found for healthy development throughout the world.

Such a programmatic framework perspective, together with the continuing day-to-day business of the global and regional power struggle, should keep any government fully occupied. But the awful truth must be faced. We cannot even begin to think of such an unfolding of foreign policy without a fundamental restructuring of internal political, economic and social policies, a restructuring which will give man the central place in planning, begin the destruction of elitism in its various aspects, and consolidate the inherent dignity of a sovereign, self-reliant nation.

The internal resurgence will have to proceed in the midst of an extraordinary change in the power balance, in ideas, concepts, values and perspectives, a change that is forced by global crises and is sweeping all the ideological fortresses of the world. The dimensions which will condition the years ahead will be made up of entirely new factors, some of which can already be seen.

1. The visible decline of the overriding economic power of the USA and an inability to halt the drift, coupled with the growth of a new capitalist philosophy which emphasizes social objectives and egalitarianism.

2. The growing managerial crisis of the socialist world (including China!), caught within its own contradictions—dialectics without dissent.

3. The fact of the sustained industrial capacity of Japan, despite a near total dependence on imported raw material, and of the European Community which is more sophisticated in many ways than other regions.

4. The rise and consolidation of a variety of multinational corporations commanding extraordinary technical and managerial skills vital to global development, and conscious of the need to de-link with obvious national interests if they are to survive.

5. The spreading realization that, to prosper, mankind will have to achieve a breakthrough in solar energy, in harnessing the resources of the oceans, in bridging global inequalities, and in curbing waste.

These five aspects of a developing situation are already intruding on the foreign policy maker wherever he or she is. The task is really to see that the institutions and instruments we possess have been so reorganized and restructured as to be able to cope with the movement of policy through this maze—for a maze it will certainly be in the foreseeable future.

24

Watershed Year*

We are in the midst of perhaps the most traumatic period in our short history as a free people. Never since the uncertain days following the partition of the subcontinent have we as a people felt so confused about the future. The familiar platitudes emanating from the labyrinth that is the Government of India, the easy rationalizations of petrified commentators, the multitude of shattering economic and political truths left unreported and unrecorded, the erosion of the moral cement binding the fragile institutions and new social practises of our infant democracy, and the persistent refusal on the part of the elite to face these facts, create the inescapable feeling that twenty-five years of effort has ended in some kind of functioning anarchy.

Such situations can continue for long stretches of time or they can be punctured with a rude suddenness. Knowing India, and the easy adaptability of our people to whatever is fated, we will plod along. However, at this juncture, it is necessary to take stock and to assess the various economic, political and social elements which will mingle to condition the dominant trends. The elements I intend to detail are not normally seen as critical. For this reason, much of the present analysis of our troubles is puerile and terribly superficial. Nineteen seventy-five is a significant watershed year, and many hitherto hidden dimensions of our situation have been sharply highlighted.

*From *Seminar*, 187; March 1975.

Over twenty-five years, as a result of uncoordinated "collaboration" agreements and a mixed economy where the boundaries of private and public responsibility were left diffused, the growing industrial base of India has not achieved the necessary balance. Self-reliance, or the capacity to grow economically with a zero input of foreign aid, has become more and more distant despite the invocations of the politicians of the Planning Commission and massive investments from many quarters.

The performance contrasts sharply with that of China. There, with a carefully balanced input of Soviet industrial muscle and extensive training, the economy has been able to generate considerable growth, ridding itself of aid and paying back debts. Chinese systems of man management are not the only explanation for the performance. The balancing of the industrial base was vital. It is not mentioned today because the Soviet contribution would then be highlighted.

The dismal failure in India to utilize anything from 50-60 per cent of the installed industrial capacity in the key areas of steel, fertilizer and power is going to compel thinking on the priority inputs needed to balance the economy. This exercise will have to be done despite the pressures of the numerous paralyzing lobbies which operate to preserve captive markets and to influence economic decisions in our country. The realization is general that the public sector is being exploited cynically by politician, bureaucrat, manager and worker. These four elements fatten on this sector at the expense of national interest. In this manner, the effort of twenty-five years has been drained out.

While the effort needed to salvage the industrial sector now enters a critical stage, and will probably see many ups and downs, the effort in agriculture fortunately achieved a significant break-through. But the hope that increased productivity on the land will deflate prices is going to be short-lived. Obviously, there is a grave underestimation of the rural determination to collect a fair price for its produce and to make the towns, which have lived on cheap food for twenty-five years, pay an economic price. The argument that this is a *kulak* demand, a demand from those who are profiteering on surpluses, fails to see that it has wide support because something of this prosperity will spill over to the more depressed sections in the countryside, creating demands and aspirations.

The inflationary price spiral has been reinforced by the swelling demand for goods from the rural areas in a period of industrial stagnation. It is short-sighted to ascribe this feature of the 1975 economic scene in India to the general price rise in the world. The repercussions are there, but India is generating its own problems. These are largely focussed on the helpless towns, for the present phase sees more money—and, with it prosperity —roaming the countryside.

Interestingly, a specific feature of the present situation is the phenomenal operation of black money and the rise of the profession of the powerfully organized smuggler, operating along India's vast coastline and, internally, along the borders of the States. The rash of corruption, now a feature of life in India, is fed by this situation and will release many new tensions and alignments in the years ahead.

Politically, it is natural to conclude that during the past twenty-five years the great democratic thrust initiated in a Hindufied society by Raja Ram Mohan Roy, which saw development under Mahatma Gandhi and its culmination in the integrated modernism of Jawaharlal Nehru, willy nilly has exhausted itself. It has been cornered and broken by revivified indigenous practice. The signs are there for all of us to see. Political management, over the last decade, has been compelled to break away from its fragile institutional moorings and has become a thing of the market place. Maybe, the age of the Pindaris is on us again and will remain with us during the years of transition to a qualitatively different social structure, evolved or born in turbulence.

Political corruption has seen a phenomenal spread during the last few years. Huge funds, created by smuggling operations, and the operations of a parallel black money economy, have made serious inroads into the management of the private and public sectors.

This hidden operation, designed originally to finance the ruling party at the Centre and now almost omnipotent in critical decision-making, has struck at the very roots of India's experiment with a just society. It rules political funds and generally creates a climate for black money. Whether it is in appointments or perks or the fixation of wages and allowances or performance norms or routine disciplines of work, the employed in India assume cynical and corrupt attitudes because of the visible degeneration around.

The political sharpening and purification which results from a principal confrontation of clearly demarcated mass formations is also not available at this critical point in our development. The ideological confusion, which resulted from the contrary pulls of a continental polity, has been heightened by the general deterioration of standards which gives the initiative to a variety of "operators." Manipulative politics by the leadership places a premium on such "operators." They have no commitments. They are wedded to their own narrow interests and have the organizational ballast to "mobilize" the masses with unaccounted funds, produced internally and also available from abroad.

Such trends are not unique in political development, but India's troubles stem from the fact that the various elements mentioned above have prevented a coherent alternative from forming. The amorphousness of the Congress Party is matched by the amorphousness of other contenders, whether communist, socialist or nationalist, rightist or leftist. In other words, the politics of consensus, so necessary in a complex federal system, has certainly lost its dynamic thrust. Clarity in national objectives has been drowned in a competing populism of the most primitive kind. And this has put the emphasis heavily on status quoism.

It is necessary to understand the meaning of status quoism in a continental situation. The ruling elites at the centre and the States are constantly working to absorb dissent and rebellion. Everyone is given a toe-hold in something or the other. Everyone is beholden to the existing system. This is not a totalitarian situation. It is a situation which in totality creates conformism or the bases of conformism for even the most uncontrollable. The consequences of this are more serious than we realize. The world is changing fast. And we are enmeshed, paralyzed, in archaic notions in the most urgent areas of decision-making.

There is grave danger that India, which at one stage attempted to chart new paths for the developing world, is in danger of being left far behind. All around us there is the evidence of a vast stirring and transformation. The ability to maintain a balanced posture when all is topsy-turvy is not to be scoffed at, but we seem to be adopting this posture on a zero rate of growth. The population explosion cannot but shatter our proverbial patience.

The social dimension of the present situation is also shot through with interesting pointers. Change of a wide-ranging kind has taken place, and is visible wherever one goes, but there has been no significant structural or qualitative change. The framework within which we function remains basically the same. The rich are richer. Comparatively, the poor are poorer. Maybe, we have graduated at the base of society from degradation to poverty, but there is small solace in this after 25 years of effort.

What continues to disturb is the polarization within our communities between what might be termed "the haves" and the "have-nots." No real communication exists between the two. It appears as if the traditional divisions of caste, particularly the brutal discriminations against the scheduled castes, were not enough to satiate the arrogance of the ruling elites. The class attitudes of the British colonialists, which compelled those lower in social status to "keep their place," have been energetically absorbed by the rising, caste-conscious middle classes of India. Socially, we have generated very unhealthy caste-cum-class attitudes, attitudes which are unfortunately unique in our region of Asia.

At the same time, almost imperceptibly, the old western-style elite, with its familiar, even rigid, Anglo-Saxon code of public posture, is disappearing. Regional elites are taking over. Rough and ready, largely rural, they are prepared for any challenge. Their behaviour pattern is naturally in collision with the old styles. Even the value systems which underpin the activities of these regional elites are very often quite different to those considered "normal." Naturally, it will take time before these patterns are accepted and integrated into the fabric of democratic functioning. The transition cannot but be somewhat tempestuous.

However, it remains to be seen how much of the breakdown in normal disciplines is a reflection of new behaviour patterns or a pointer to impatience with political, economic and social status quoism. The entire spectrum of public and private activity is affected by a growing anarchy fed by the populist propaganda of short-sighted politicians. The normal equations of class confrontation do not apply, for the employed of India are privileged by the very fact of their employment. Every attempt by the employed to increase their slice of the cake affects the resources for further development. In other words, the battle to reduce inequalities has to apply to the nation as a whole, not to the tiny employed minority. This aspect of the struggle is deliberately underplayed by the politicians of various parties and the leaders of trade unions, largely because they have not been able to integrate their notions of socialism with the specific conditions in India. This failure is destroying the catalytic role of the public sector in particular.

The extraordinary rise in prices, coupled with the prevailing inability to make the system function at some degree of efficiency, has further eroded the potential for collective action—and even the desire to think in terms of a collective conscience. Without such psychological preparation, it is not possible to plan or implement any major developmental thrusts which help to make up the leeway of centuries. We are in the midst of a terrible revival of individualism, popularized essentially by a manipulative political leadership which is fearful of institutional mandates or direction by the party organization.

The more perceptive are at last beginning to realize that only a major overhaul of the framework within which we have been functioning is now on the agenda. The delay in facing this challenge embedded in old notions of economics and politics, of the meaning of change, is intensifying the crisis which surrounds us. We need to clean our brains of the cobwebs which prevent us from seeing the qualitatively new elements which are shaping the future. Wherever one goes in India, there is a deep reluctance to adjust to the essence of this challenge.

Reluctantly or otherwise, we will have to work out a mass line for the upliftment of our people. We will have to find the short cuts to reach standards of living which are dignified and waste-free. The challenge is wide ranging, almost forbidding, but it has to be met. And, let us be clear, there are no answers in the easy slogans of the free enterprise and planned societies. Values are under debate, values which underpin civilizations. We cannot run away from this debate. Then, there will be no short cut—only a maze, a baffling maze.

If 1975 has become a watershed year for us, it marks a major turning point in the life of a world in the throes of production and consumption problems the like of which have not been known. Clearly, the way we are going as earthlings invites only complications and traumas. But no one anywhere can as yet see the practical alternative, or even the faint outlines of such an alternative. This absence of an alternative keeps us functioning within the frame of value systems which we know are self defeating. At this moment in our scientific-technological mastery, we find ourselves powerless to build an intelligent rational model of all-round universal growth. This is the crisis. And we are very much one of the major focii of it.

All the more reason, then, that we begin to shake-up our local system of thought and action. Only through such an indigenous shake-up, a process of trial and error, will we be able to cut through some of the confusion. The more we pioneer, the more we experiment, the better. That is the lesson we have to learn from this watershed year.

25

Strategy for Tomorrow*

In a sense, this is the wrong time to talk about strategies for India. Everything seems to be out of joint, as it were. Production is at a standstill. Prices are shooting. Inflation is rampant. Industry is mismanaged. Corruption is eating into the vitals of our society. Drought has played havoc with our reserves of food. The politican is adding fuel to the fire, confusion to the chaos. And our population continues to boom. All this notwithstanding, it is at moments such as these that we need to take stock of what we have done, and to re-plan our efforts to become a sovereign, self-reliant, dignified people.

If we think in terms of a strategy for tomorrow, we must project ourselves forward into the kind of problems we will be facing at the turn of the century. The seventies become relevant in the next twenty-five year stretch. Imagine the situation in the year 2000. And I will refer to only one fact which we will be living with at the end of the next twenty-five years. There will be anything from 800 million to 1000 million Indians inhabiting this subcontinent. We need to let this fact sink in— or else the strategy I talk about will not make sense.

We have arrived at a point in our history when the dream that inspired us in the building of our society is dissolving. We clutch at an achievement here or an achievement there, but we are unable to see the way to raise our people to a dignified life.

*From a talk, January 1975.

In other words, we have not failed, but we seem to have gone wrong somewhere. The emphasis was incorrect, unreal. We have, as it were, grown within the old framework—modified here and there, but still the old framework. And yet we had planned and worked for a major break through which would help us, as Nehru used to say, to make up the leeway of centuries.

We have grown in capacity and affluence. We have grown to command tasks which our forefathers never dreamt of. Others have risen from the dust and proved their mettle against the best of this world. The patterns of poverty have changed. Our horizons, intellectual and spiritual, have been transformed. But, and this is the point I want to stress, we remain very much a slow-moving, status quoist society. Some forty per cent of our population continues to live in the gravest condition. Another thirty per cent is moving towards security, but a single drought can reduce them to quarry workers. The administrators, the academicians, the technicians, the managers, the professionals, the skilled workers are the remaining thirty per cent—and the future depends largely on how they move to shape it. Their ideas, attitudes and value systems—conscious and unconscious— make the strategy for tomorrow. It is here that the intellectual attack has to be concentrated.

In our sprawling, multi-cultural and much varied subcontinent, we have to evolve a policy which will dissolve the extraordinary gulf that exists between the elite and the mass of the people, the rich and the poor, the town-dweller and the villager, the upper crust and the lowest of the low—a policy which will in the *shortest possible time* lift the Indian people from depravity to poverty, and from poverty to dignity. In such a society, affluence must be fought as a criminal waste, as the life style of those who lack a conscience. This will have to be the kernel of the strategy if we wish to avoid the familiar path of violence and revolution which could dismember our delicate federal polity.

I believe that it is possible to cut this path to the future, that it is not some idealistic dream. Indeed, with the world's total resources seriously depleted some such thoughts are beginning to stir even in those advanced societies which have established the false standards we seem so desperately anxious to imitate.

Over the past twenty-five years of freedom, we have managed to build up an agricultural and industrial infrastructure which can yield immense dividends. The talent and skill also exists for a major transformation. If we have failed to organize an egalitarian, hard-headed, disciplined society it is because we could not organize a collective will, a collective conscience. The quest for private profit, for personal advancement, for individual ambitions, could not be broken or replaced—indeed, the institutions of colonialism and the natural impulses of a largely middle-class-directed freedom movement strengthened the individualistic elitist tendencies. Today, we are compelled to swim with this current even as we try to discipline it. I say this despite all the radical talk we hear these days about transforming our society.

To make the debate on strategies clear, it is necessary to present a somewhat complex exercise. It will confine myself largely to economics and politics. All else flows from here. I shall attempt to sketch what should have been done. Then, following the failures inherent in the past 25 years of planning, to pose the kind of choices we have to make even as we rely on private effort to boost the developmental effort. Wrong choices could take us into a maze from which it would be difficult to extricate ourselves without a costly revolution.

Gandhi preceded Mao. Without any doubt he was the most perceptive of our leaders. He understood the raw reality that is India, understood the need for creative, and even unique, answers to problems facing us. He certainly struck a deep chord in the India psyche. He was a man of fifty when he arrived in India from South Africa, without the usual charismatic traits, preaching the strange gospel of *satyagraha* against one of the most experienced of world imperialisms, without mass media, without the usual paraphernalia of party machines. The man was a phenomenon in his country—and outside. He moulded the ethos of an entire movement. And yet he was forgotten within months of the transfer of power, forgotten in the sense that nothing of his unique approach to problems was absorbed by the policy makers of free India. Recipients of a ravaged, partitioned inheritance, these policy makers pursued a stereo-typed path of development—a mix of the practices of free enterprising capitalist and autocratic egalitarian societies. The mix has not worked. I will not go into all the details. Suffice it to say that at the core of the problem lies the failure of the public sector, both as a productive sector and as a sector which commands the heights of the economy, conditioning the patterns of growth. The public sector, into which was invested the saving and resource of 25 years, was blatantly exploited by both managers and working force without any disciplined effort at increased productivity. Indeed, hardly 35-40 per cent of the installed capacities are being utilized in many critical areas and often less. This shocking misuse of public funds was further aggravated by diverting the production of the public sector into the manufacture of luxury goods for the urban population. We needed to establish strict priorities for the "forced march" to industrialization which so many had talked about. Apart from a few perceptive thinkers, no one referred to this great betrayal of economic goals.

Today, after twenty-five years, the theory is naturally being trotted out that the public sector is a failure, and that only the private sector, relieved of restrictions, rules, regulations and inhibitions can deliver the goods. And the demoralization about government's economic efforts, together with the realization that chaotic situations prevail in so many corporations, is so widespread that the public is prepared to listen. This is a sad commentary on our handling of our economic condition. We are in reverse gear. Yet, I think, there are possibilities of immense improvement in performance and perspective even as we enter this confused transition to what might well become an Indian capitalist-socialist path with its own special features.

One can almost hear the leadership of the ruling party, saying that this development will be rigorously controlled. We can only hope that this will not mean another package of so-called controls, more honoured in the breach than in the observance, a network of patronage and corruption. This would only result in a continuing paralysis on the production front. Then again, we hope that the law of the jungle will not prevail. Unbridled free enterprise in a continental economy like ours would result in grave imbalances and a politically explosive situation. Indeed, the crises of today would return after a decade in more vicious form. In other words, while welcoming growth by whichever means we can achieve it, it is fundamental to our general well-being that the *content of this* growth be carefully controlled. There can be growth and growth. We must work for growth that humanizes our society, that reduces the violent tensions within it, that liberates the initiative of men and organizations. Now this often sounds like some kind of mumbo-jumbo. Let me tell you broadly what I expect of economic growth in the seventies in India.

Insted of talking about minimum needs, we must set-up the *maxima*, the level to which we want to take our entire society. Maxima also means that anything beyond is waste. It gives us a clear perspective about resources, consumption needs and standards of living-matters over which there is much manipulated confusion. This is the dynamic of a new living standard.

Instead of wasting our limited resources of cement and steel, needed for priority tasks, the millions of India should be housed in local materials of which properly treated mud is traditional. The best designers and architects should be put to work on local materials to create new habitats, properly served by water and drainage, built to last for a few years, but easily rebuilt and remodelled. In this way, the millions of India would resume a certain part of their lost dignity within a single five-year plan. This is the dynamic of mass housing.

Instead of expending limited medical facilities on serving the superannuated in the cities, the country should be criss-crossed by dispensaries and first aid posts stocked with the pills and powders which take care of nearly ninety per cent of the diseases and ailments afflicting the people. Sophisticated medical support can only be built on such a base. This is the dynamic of mass health.

Instead of programmes to create the educated unemployed of India, the schooling and university system should be drastically overhauled to serve those sectors of our growing economy which require trained manpower. The situation today is without priorities and without perspectives. Education has become a farce, and the campus a septic focus infecting the body politic. What we need is a trained manpower plan. Anyone making the grade should be guaranteed a job. This could at least provide a beginning to an urgent revolution—the dynamic of mass education.

Instead of creating urban slums, rapid mass transport systems have to be organized to bring the living areas in the countryside into contact with places of work and study and trade. Slum creation in over-populated condition would mean deadly cities of 20 to 30 million each. Efficient transport opens up the countryside and breaks the obsession with the private automobile now choking the streets of advanced cities—the dynamic of mass transport.

Instead of imitation, the stress should shift to a total restructuring of ideas and concepts. Value systems must undergo fundamental transformation—and with these transformations, the power system will come under basic review. Maybe, a beginning will be in the field of culture where the clash between modernism and tradition is basically a reflection of the economic polarization. In other words, tradition must become an integral part of the modern infrastructure. This is the dynamic of a mass society which shuns elitism.

These are some of the economic thrusts within a changed value system. I say "some" because the moment we start thinking in this new context, the whole planning process will come under fundamental review. The vested economic interest inherent in the old structure has to be broken by a determined leadership. The moment this process is initiated, it is inevitable that the effect will be felt in the political and social spheres.

For example, take the area of implementation. It demands a system of decentralization, a delegation of authority in decision-making and financial funding. Fundamental transformations cannot be carried out from distant Delhi. Delhi has to take the key decisions, but must rely on a widespread initiative for implementation—and this will not evolve without a widespread decentralization of authority. And as decentralization comes on to the agenda in an urgent form, the whole question of giant monolithic linguistic States will be spot-lighted. They will be seen as the anachronisms they are. Giganticism, unless absolutely necessary, is an enemy of human dignity, of human involvement and initiative.

We are already nearly half way through the seventies—that is, if you consider that the general elections are only a year away, and also remember that "strategies" for national coherence and development cannot be worked in haste. Too many sensitive factors are involved and have to be commanded with care and persuasion. In other words, the politics of economics have to be kept in mind.

I have already referred to decentralization and to the need to divide the subcontinent into smaller, more coherent States. Exercises along these lines have been done and India emerges as a federation of some 50-60 States. It is always maintained that the cost of such a reorganization is forbidding. This thought occurs because people forget the cost of inefficient, large States, the cost of political factions and instability and the psychological cost of more powerful segments exploiting the less powerful in the existing States. In the seventies, we will realize the truth that there is good sense in having more States. And a certain economic prosperity will provide an easier atmosphere for the operation. It remains to be seen whether we will be able to carry through in maturity this reorganization of our life and politics.